IDIOT'S
GUIDES
AS EASY AS IT

Tarot

by Avia Venefica

ALPHA

A member of Penguin Group (USA) Inc.

ALPHA BOOKS

Published by Penguin Group (USA) Inc.

Penguin Group (USA) Inc., 375 Hudson Street, New York, New York 10014, USA · Penguin Group (Canada), 90 Eglinton Avenue East, Suite 700, Toronto, Ontario M4P 2Y3, Canada (a division of Pearson Penguin Canada Inc.) · Penguin Books Ltd., 80 Strand, London WC2R 0RL, England · Penguin Ireland, 25 St. Stephen's Green, Dublin 2, Ireland (a division of Penguin Books Ltd.) · Penguin Group (Australia), 250 Camberwell Road, Camberwell, Victoria 3124, Australia (a division of Pearson Australia Group Pty. Ltd.) · Penguin Books India Pvt. Ltd., 11 Community Centre, Panchsheel Park, New Delhi—110 017, India · Penguin Group (NZ), 67 Apollo Drive, Rosedale, North Shore, Auckland 1311, New Zealand (a division of Pearson New Zealand Ltd.) · Penguin Books (South Africa) (Pty.) Ltd., 24 Sturdee Avenue, Rosebank, Johannesburg 2196, South Africa · Penguin Books Ltd., Registered Offices: 80 Strand, London WC2R 0RL, England

International Standard Book Number: 978-1-61564-499-5
Library of Congress Catalog Card Number: 2013956271

16   15   14   8   7   6   5   4   3   2   1

Interpretation of the printing code: The rightmost number of the first series of numbers is the year of the book's printing; the rightmost number of the second series of numbers is the number of the book's printing. For example, a printing code of 14-1 shows that the first printing occurred in 2014.

Note: This publication contains the opinions and ideas of its author. It is intended to provide helpful and informative material on the subject matter covered. It is sold with the understanding that the author and publisher are not engaged in rendering professional services in the book. If the reader requires personal assistance or advice, a competent professional should be consulted. The author and publisher specifically disclaim any responsibility for any liability, loss, or risk, personal or otherwise, which is incurred as a consequence, directly or indirectly, of the use and application of any of the contents of this book.

Most Alpha books are available at special quantity discounts for bulk purchases for sales promotions, premiums, fund-raising, or educational use. Special books, or book excerpts, can also be created to fit specific needs. For details, write: Special Markets, Alpha Books, 375 Hudson Street, New York, NY 10014.

Trademarks: All terms mentioned in this book that are known to be or are suspected of being trademarks or service marks have been appropriately capitalized. Alpha Books and Penguin Group (USA) Inc. cannot attest to the accuracy of this information. Use of a term in this book should not be regarded as affecting the validity of any trademark or service mark.

Publisher: *Mike Sanders*
Executive Managing Editor: *Billy Fields*
Acquisitions Editor: *Karyn Gerhard*
Senior Development Editor: *Megan Douglass*
Senior Production Editor: *Janette Lynn*

Cover/Book Designer: *Rebecca Batchelor*
Indexer: *Ginny Bess Munroe*
Layout: *Ayanna Lacey*
Proofreader: *Laura Caddell*

This book is dedicated to you, dear reader.
May your cards be bright and your
path filled with light.

CONTENTS

THE BEGINNING........3

ABOUT THE TAROT DECK ... 4

INTUITION, ALLEGORY,
AND DIALOGUE 6

HOW TO USE THIS BOOK..... 8

A GLOSSARY OF
TAROT-RELATED TERMS ...10

THE CARDS.............13

INTRODUCTION AND
EXPLANATION 14

THE MAJOR ARCANA........19

The Fool 20

The Magician 22

The High Priestess 24

The Empress...................... 26

The Emperor 28

The Hierophant.................... 30

The Lovers....................... 32

The Chariot...................... 34

Strength 36

The Hermit 38

Wheel of Fortune 40

Justice 42

The Hanged Man 44

Death 46

Temperance 48

The Devil 50

The Tower 52

The Star......................... 54

The Moon........................ 56

The Sun.......................... 58

Judgment 60

The World 62

THE SUIT OF WANDS........65

ACE of Wands 66

TWO of Wands 68

THREE of Wands................... 70

FOUR of Wands 72

FIVE of Wands 74

SIX of Wands 76

SEVEN of Wands................... 78

EIGHT of Wands 80

NINE of Wands..................... 82

TEN of Wands 84

PAGE of Wands..................... 86

KNIGHT of Wands 88

QUEEN of Wands 90

KING of Wands..................... 92

THE SUIT OF PENTACLES ..95

ACE of Pentacles 96

TWO of Pentacles 98

THREE of Pentacles.............. 100

FOUR of Pentacles 102

FIVE of Pentacles 104

SIX of Pentacles 106

SEVEN of Pentacles............... 108

EIGHT of Pentacles 110

NINE of Pentacles................. 112

TEN of Pentacles 114

PAGE of Pentacles................. 116

KNIGHT of Pentacles 118

QUEEN of Pentacles 120

KING of Pentacles................. 122

THE SUIT OF SWORDS..... 125

ACE of Swords..................... 126

TWO of Swords.................... 128

THREE of Swords 130

FOUR of Swords................... 132

FIVE of Swords 134

SIX of Swords...................... 136

SEVEN of Swords 138

EIGHT of Swords.................. 140

NINE of Swords 142

TEN of Swords 144

PAGE of Swords 146

KNIGHT of Swords................ 148

QUEEN of Swords................. 150

KING of Swords 152

THE SUIT OF CUPS.........155

ACE of Cups 156

TWO of Cups 158

THREE of Cups.................... 160

FOUR of Cups 162

FIVE of Cups 164

SIX of Cups 166

SEVEN of Cups 168

EIGHT of Cups 170

NINE of Cups...................... 172

TEN of Cups 174

PAGE of Cups...................... 176

KNIGHT of Cups 178

QUEEN of Cups 180

KING of Cups...................... 182

READING THE CARDS 185

READING BASICS 187

CARD POSITIONS 190

HOW TO ASK QUESTIONS WITH THE TAROT 192

GETTING ANSWERS WITH THE TAROT 194

HANDLING THE CARDS ... 188

DOING READINGS 198

THE 4 BASIC SPREADS 203

BASIC SPREAD #1: PAST, PRESENT, FUTURE 204

BASIC SPREAD #2: DAILY ENCOUNTER 208

BASIC SPREAD #3: TAKE ACTION 212

BASIC SPREAD #4: THE MODIFIED CROSS ... 216

SPREADS FOR SPECIFIC QUESTIONS 223

FINANCIAL FORECAST SPREAD 224

LOVE AND RELATIONSHIPS SPREAD 230

WHOLE HEALTH REPORT SPREAD 238

APPENDIXES 245

FREQUENTLY ASKED QUESTIONS AND TAROT TROUBLESHOOTING 246

TAROT SYMBOLISM 250

INDEX 260

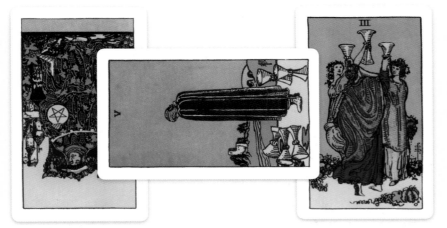

INTRODUCTION

I love a good mystery. In my opinion, there's no greater mystery than the sacred wisdom tucked within the cards of the Tarot. Cracking the secrets of the Tarot is what prompted me to get my first deck. I couldn't have chosen a better mystery to solve!

I like to think of the Tarot as a higher calling. Perhaps you love a good mystery, too. Maybe you feel inexplicably drawn to the power of the Tarot. Maybe you have a feeling that life is multi-dimensional, and recognize the Tarot as an exciting way to access those many dimensions. Whatever your reasons for learning about this unique system of wisdom—I'm under the belief you were called to the Tarot.

I was called to the Tarot around the age of twelve. I'd always been imaginative and the Tarot was a perfect addition to my dreamy world. I was completely enchanted by its odd imagery and secret meanings. It wasn't long before I became an avid student of the Tarot. I consumed loads of texts and resources on the Tarot to learn everything I could about it. More than 20 years later, I'm still learning. That's the beauty of the Tarot. It has limitless potential, and its wisdom unfolds as we grow and evolve with it.

Like most people who first come to the Tarot, the only thing I knew about it was what I'd seen on TV and in movies. I quickly learned there was infinitely more depth and purpose to the Tarot than just using it as a fortune-telling tool or a hokey Halloween parlor trick.

That's why I was so jazzed about writing this book. I felt it was an opportunity to dispel some of the hype and nonsense the media tends to spin about the cards. My sincere intent with this book is to present the Tarot as a diverse system of knowledge that is as flexible as you need it to be. I want to convey to you, dear reader, that the Tarot is a partner on your life-path. It will grow as you grow, and Tarot has the ability to enhance your life in tremendous ways.

My genuine hope is that this book is just the first leg on your Tarot journey. If I've done my job right, this book will encourage you to keep learning about the Tarot, its many uses, and how it can enrich your life. If you stick with it, the Tarot can be an amazing helper that can engage you in a lifelong adventure of self-discovery.

You can learn more about me and my experience with the Tarot by visiting my website, www.TarotTeachings. com. You can also visit my main website, www.Whats-Your-Sign.com, for insights into the wonderful world of symbolic meanings.

ACKNOWLEDGMENTS

It's been said that no man is an island. This is certainly the case with me and writing this book. I owe a great deal of gratitude to several people who were crucial in the process and completion of this project.

Although not directly involved in the writing process, I have to thank my family for their endless support and encouragement. On your Tarot journey, you may run into some negative attitudes about the Tarot. My family is very committed to their faith, and they could have easily snubbed their noses at my acceptance to write a book about the Tarot. Thankfully, they kept their minds open, and their hearts kind. Their love for me far outweighed any misgivings they may have had about the Tarot and my involvement with it. For that, I'm infinitely grateful. Thanks mom, dad, and sis for always being in my corner, and loving me no matter how "out there" I get.

My dear friend Lynn King was incredibly supportive in writing this book, too. Even in the midst of relocating to a new home, being a mother of two beautiful children, and meeting the demands of her professional career, Lynn took the time to help me. Her revisions and suggestions were invaluable. I count this book as a success partly because of Lynn's savvy, smart observations.

Last, but hardly least, I have to thank my partner Dave Crotty for his ceaseless support. Dave read each and every word of this book with an objective, intelligent eye. Dave was instrumental in simplifying my often overcomplicated and potentially verbose writing style. There were some hairy moments in writing this book, and Dave was my wingman the whole way. His strength and support kept me clear from several crash and burn moments. Thanks, Dave, for keeping me sane and focused and for being my best mate.

THE BEGINNING

ABOUT THE TAROT DECK

Whether for idle curiosity or serious research, odds are you picked up this book because you're looking for answers. The Tarot and this book can offer a wealth of insight into your questions, though the Tarot and its origins are cloaked in mystery.

To begin, there are no absolute answers about the origin of the Tarot. Tarot is a collection of many spiritual philosophies. Take a look at the cards and observe the cultural diversity reflected in its imagery. You can see influences from Egypt, Judaism, Western astrology, alchemy, and the Christian Bible in some of the deck's symbolism.

In its infancy, the Tarot may have started as tiles from Asia with etchings of pictures and symbols to predict the future. From there, the images likely migrated to Persia or Arabia. Scholars postulate the first standardized Tarot-like system was introduced to Europe (probably via the spice trade routes) in the 1300s. Along the way, each culture added its own philosophical spin to the Tarot. In essence, the Tarot is a melting pot of global wisdom with each civilization contributing to its value.

The Tarot's author remains anonymous, too. Great minds and artists (such as Arthur Waite and Aleister Crowley) have improved upon the deck over the centuries, but the master who first created the Tarot is still a mystery.

If you think about it, life itself is also a mystery. The Tarot is a response to age-old questions humankind has asked since the dawn of time. Simply put, the Tarot is a system of wisdom similar to other sacred texts that offer guidance on a spiritual level. Like most sacred wisdom, its mystery is purposeful. The Tarot offers partial answers, because it requires *your* participation in order to create "big picture" solutions. The elusive quality of the Tarot is designed to get you thinking and searching your heart for the other half of the equations you seek to solve.

Speaking of solving problems, most people think the Tarot is a way to tell the future. Although Tarot does reveal patterns that unfold into logical outcomes to your future, its value goes far beyond that. Because the Tarot is an account of life's diversity, its uses are equally diverse. From dream interpretation, to family counseling, the Tarot is as flexible as you need it to be.

Actually, the Tarot is used by many professionals for insight, inspiration, and ideas. Many professional writers glean character traits and story lines from the Tarot. Artists often rely on Tarot to stimulate creativity. Even some reputable psychologists use the Tarot in their field. Dr. Carl Jung, a renowned psychologist and psychotherapist, employed the Tarot in his research with groundbreaking results.

In fact, Dr. Jung recognized Tarot's importance in his work with archetypes. An archetype is an idea, image, or thought that is shared by all humankind throughout history. For example, the concept of "hero" is something all humans are familiar with; every culture identifies with the hero archetype and relates to his/her qualities of bravery, strength, and valor.

The Tarot reveals archetypes, which is why it can be a tool for prediction and problem solving. Why? Because every human is unique, but the human experience is common; we all share similar emotions and patterns in our lives. The Tarot simply lays out these patterns in front of us so we can connect the dots and formulate our next step on the journey of life.

Your unique experiences and vision are the reason the Tarot comes to life as a guide. Your own thoughts and needs will clarify and illuminate the cards you draw. The cards you draw, individually and as a grouping, will give clarity to your current condition and will offer guidance through patterns for how you should respond to your circumstances. Just remember, the Tarot is a reflection. You are the source. Together, you and the Tarot can be a great team in gaining insight, wisdom, and clarity about anything you can imagine.

INTUITION, ALLEGORY, AND DIALOGUE:
TAROT AND THE STORY OF YOU!

The Tarot is remarkably effective in understanding your life—who you are and what to do about your life. Using the Tarot for clarification in these areas requires an open mind and heart. This can only be done through earnest pursuit of self-truth and willingness to understand the story of your life; the good, bad, and everything in between.

TAROT AS ALLEGORY

When you read a story, your imagination conjures images based on the descriptions and details you're reading. Reading the Tarot works the same way, only you are using your imagination and intuition to formulate details and descriptions about your life story.

The Tarot is like an allegory. An allegory is a picture or story on the surface, but it carries a hidden meaning; there is always a message or moral to be found. The Tarot cards you pull for yourself in a reading tell the story about you. Your creativity, imagination, and intuition will uncover the hidden lessons behind your life's circumstances.

The Tarot has a whole cast of characters, each with their own personality and message. As with any good allegory, paying attention to the dialogue between the characters is key to gleaning vital clues to the story. When you lay the cards out in a reading, try to imagine the characters in the cards speaking to you and to one another. What are they saying? What messages are the characters conveying to each other and to you?

USING YOUR INTUITION

Intuition is your most important tool for interpreting the story the Tarot is telling you. Have you ever acted on a feeling or had a hunch you couldn't explain, but it just felt right? That's your intuition stirring within you. You are far more than your body and brain. There is a superior guidance system that dwells within you. Tapping into your intuitive guidance system opens up a whole new dimension of understanding and perception.

Intuition is a special kind of intelligence. If you have a math problem you use your analytical, logical mind to solve it. Reading the Tarot is like solving a math problem, but instead of working with numbers, you are dealing with the complexities of your life. Your life is an equation, and you will rely on your creative, intuitive self to get answers with the Tarot.

ACCESSING YOUR INTUITION

So how do you access your intuitive self? Because intuition is not based on logic, you will have to find ways to suspend literal thinking and reasoning. The trick to tapping into your intuition is distracting the analytical mind. If you meditate, this is an excellent way to prepare your intuition before a reading. If not, try closing your eyes, and coax your awareness into a dreamy state. Focus on your breathing and let your consciousness drift in a relaxed, free-flowing manner.

Experiment with techniques to bypass your logic and move into your intuition. Practice and patience will yield great results. Your intuition is not something to be obtained; you already have it, you just need to find ways to access it.

HOW TO USE THIS BOOK

The beauty of the Tarot is that it's highly customizable. The more you familiarize yourself with the cards, the more personal your experience with the Tarot will be. This book is merely the starting point in your *evolving* relationship with the Tarot. Ideally, your understanding of yourself and the cards will grow, leading to rich and enlightening experiences with the Tarot.

This book offers basic information to get you started with the Tarot as simply and quickly as possible. Once you have the basics of this book under your belt, you may desire to add your own meanings and interpretations. This is a natural progression as you spend more time exploring the cards.

THE CARDS

The card images in this book are from the Rider-Waite deck. This deck, created by Arthur Edward Waite, is one of the most standardized decks on the market, and is most commonly used today. There are hundreds of versions of the Tarot, many of which mimic the core elements of the Rider-Waite deck. You may want to look into different decks after you become more familiar with the Rider-Waite.

Interpreting the Cards

Suggested interpretations for each card are broken into sections for quick reference: Keywords, Core Meanings, Quick-Read Meanings, Key Questions, and a "The Card Says" section to round out the personality of each card.

The message for each card differs depending on whether the card is upright, or upside down (reversed). Keywords and meanings are given for both upright, and reversed positions.

The Keywords for each card are a quick reference concerning the main issues expressed in that card. It might be helpful to memorize these Keywords as you learn the cards. Recalling one or two Keywords may help trigger your memory on other details about the card.

The Core Meaning section gives you a summary, and establishes the primary theme for each card.

The Quick-Read Meanings are responses to some of the most common concerns in every human life: love, money, career, and family. For example, if you're perplexed about your job, you can pull a card with that question in mind and refer directly to the career portion of the Quick-Read Meanings.

The Key Questions section is particularly useful because it prompts you to ask yourself questions to which the answers can be intensely revealing. These questions are designed to initiate a truthful dialogue with your inner self. Each card poses a question in such a candid way; it's like having a supportive friend to help you uncover a secret truth within you.

Lastly, the "The Card Says" section is written as if the card is speaking directly to you. Each statement is no-nonsense, straight-shooting advice.

CARD READINGS

The section of this book titled "Reading the Cards" gives suggestions on how to handle the cards when shuffling and pulling them from the deck. It also covers basics on asking questions, and how to create a spread for your readings.

How you use this book will depend on your approach to learning. Some of you will want to dive right in by laying out your first spread and start reading the cards. If this is you, go ahead and lay out a few cards, then consult the sections of this book to help with your interpretations. Others will want to methodically visit each card and evaluate its meaning. If this is you, study each card in conjunction with the meanings in this book, then move on for guidance on doing your first readings.

Either way, you will find this book to be a comprehensive and insightful reference as you begin your Tarot adventures. Consider this book your first step on a remarkable journey of learning and discovery.

A GLOSSARY OF
TAROT-RELATED TERMS

affirmation   A statement (usually positive) that is repeated with the goal of reprogramming the mind and its belief systems. Tarot imagery can be used in conjunction with affirmations in order to solidify meaning within the psyche.

allegory   An allegory is a picture or story that carries a hidden meaning. There is always a message or moral to be learned from an allegory. For example, allegory in The Hanged Man card conveys a message of letting go, or suspending control.

arcana   This is Latin for "secret" or "mystery." The Tarot is comprised of a Major Arcana and a Minor Arcana. As you might guess, the Major Arcana reveals big mysteries. The Minor Arcana offers clues about smaller, simpler secrets in your life. Arcana is plural, arancum is singular.

archetype   A term coined by Dr. Carl Jung to describe imagery, personalities, and experiences common among all humans. For example, the concept of "hero" is an archetype. Throughout all cultures, the hero archetype stands for courage and bravery. The cards of the Tarot are based on archetypes. One example of this is The Lovers , which illustrates the archetypal experience of love.

divination   A Latin term from the word *divinus* which means "to be inspired by the divine." The Tarot is a form of divination because its sacred wisdom and imagery is designed to inspire you to unite with divine intuition for illumination about life.

esoteric   Knowledge that is ancient, secret, or not commonly known. Tarot is considered to be esoteric because it is based on secret knowledge reserved for a select few who desire to learn its mysteries.

initiate   A person who is starting on a learning path into a specialized, esoteric wisdom. A student of the Tarot is often referred to as an initiate.

intuition   Knowing and/or insight that is obtained by means other than intellect or reason; instinctive perception. Intuition is a critical skill employed when reading and working with the Tarot.

LWB or **LBB**   This is an abbreviation commonly used in the Tarot community. It refers to the "Little White Book" or "Little Black Book" included with every Tarot deck. These small books typically give definitions and information about the deck.

meditation   A process of relaxing the body, mind, and spirit. Meditating before reading Tarot frees your intuitive self which is vital in obtaining meaningful, soulful readings.

occult   Mass media and stereotypical judgments have given this term some negative connotations, but it really just means "hidden." In truth, the word refers to things that are mysterious and supernatural. The Tarot is considered an occult system of wisdom because its truths are cloaked in mystery.

oracle   A person or device that delivers profound, accurate, and wise projections. An oracle taps into higher wisdom and intuition to deliver insightful revelations. The Tarot is considered an oracle. If a Tarot reader is connected to a higher source of knowledge (intuition, spiritual energy, etc.) then he/she may also be considered an oracle of wisdom.

pips   A Tarot term that refers to the cards in the Minor Arcana.

projective hand   This is your dominant hand. If you are right-handed, that is your projective hand. This hand gives out energy. Use this hand to move your intuitive energy out from yourself and through the Tarot. This hand is used when pulling the cards and forming them in a spread. In essence this hand is a natural pathway to send out your energy into the cards or to your querent. *See also* receptive hand.

querent   If you are reading for others, the querent is the person for whom you are reading the Tarot.

receptive hand   This is your non-dominant hand. If you are right-handed, then your left hand is your receptive hand. This hand receives energy. Use this hand to receive intuitive energy from the Tarot. This hand is used when initially handling the cards (shuffling and cutting). This hand is an energetic channel that allows you to take in intuitive information. *See also* projective hand.

significator   This card is assigned an exclusive position in your readings that signifies you. The card pulled and placed in a signifier position will represent you; where you are in life; and what your current emotional, physical, and/or mental status is. If reading for others, the significator represents your querent.

smudging   This is a ceremonial practice for cleansing the cards. This practice is conducted by some Tarot readers in order to rid the cards of residual energy from previous uses. White sage is a common smudging tool, but you can use your favorite incense.

spread   This is the formation of the cards laid out before you. A spread is the most common way of reading the cards. Spreads are also referred to as layouts.

trumps   This is a term that refers to the cards in the Major Arcana.

THE CARDS

THE CARDS:
INTRODUCTION AND EXPLANATION

The Tarot deck is comprised of two main sections: Major Arcana and Minor Arcana. The word *arcana* means "secret" or "mystery."

The Major Arcana (or "big mystery") has 22 cards. These cards are major players on the stage of your readings. They reveal powerful truths and represent big issues. The Major Arcana reflects long-term, deep-seated aspects of your life.

The Minor Arcana (or "small mystery") has 56 cards. These cards talk about the small issues you deal with in your life. They address common, day-to-day aspects of your experience.

Think of the cards spread out before you like characters in a play. The Major Arcana cards are the lead actors, whereas the Minor Arcana cards take on supporting roles.

FOUR SUITS OF THE MINOR ARCANA

Within the Minor Arcana are four suits: Wands, Pentacles, Swords, and Cups. Each suit is connected to an element: Fire, Earth, Air, and Water (respectively). These elements are important to know because they are the prime building blocks of life. Memorizing the elements that go with each suit will give you a foundational meaning for that card. For example, all pentacles are associated with earth, so you know you are dealing with material, earthy matters when these cards pop up in a reading. Here are some overarching themes of the four suits in the Minor Arcana. These themes will help you understand the flavor of the suits and bring meaning to your readings.

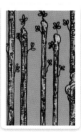

Wands

This suit is connected with the element of **fire**. As a fire symbol, wands represent heat, passion, and creativity. When wands show up in your readings, be mindful of burning desires, and that which sparks your creativity. Think about what kindles and ignites passion in your life. Whether music or social gatherings, wands will point to actions that light you up.

Swords

Swords are aligned with the element of **air**. This symbol slices through the unseen realms of thought. Consider energy and data transferred through the air via radio waves and cell phone towers. Swords illustrate mental energy and intellectual concentration, and often reveal disturbances of the mind or mental preoccupations. Swords offer guidance about issues that hold your attention (or cause worry and stress).

Pentacles

Pentacles represent the element of **earth**. They deal with being grounded, and this translates to themes of money, home, and materialism. Pentacle cards are often referred to as "money cards" and give insight into financial issues. They can also give a glimpse into material gain, especially concerning home life. Whatever represents value, stability, and security will be revealed by the suit of pentacles.

Cups

The suit of cups is associated with the element of **water**. Water deals with emotion and intuition. Consider what water does: it flows, cleans, and fills. The cups suit is often referred to as the suit of "love cards," as they commonly give insight into this emotion. When you pull cups in a reading, you are dealing with purification of feelings, the flow of emotion, and clearness of intuition.

GETTING TO KNOW THE ROYAL FAMILY

Also known as court cards, the royals of the Tarot are: Page, Knight, Queen, and King. Each of the four suits feature these nobles. Unless expressly positioned in a reading as yourself, the court cards most likely represent friends, family, and co-workers and the important roles they play in your life.

The following guidelines will help you pinpoint personality types of the court cards, helping you to identify who they are, what they're telling you, and what roles they play in your life.

Pages

These are people who are on the path of learning. They seek to better understand their world. These are often young people who are developing themselves or their sense of self. Pages are often under the authority of others. They are heavily influenced by people around them because they haven't developed their identities enough to take action for themselves. Pages are a work in progress. They can be free spirits and sometimes confused about their direction.

- Personality traits: childlike, trusting, willing, helpful, seeking, impulsive, playful

- Gender: male or female or androgynous (a person who expresses both genders equally)

- Age group: children, or people with a childlike demeanor

Knights

These personality types are about action and taking charge. They have developed a sense of purpose, and are often on a mission or lofty quest. These are the movers and shakers in your life. They seem to have boundless energy and passion for a cause. Knights represent people who know what they want and aren't afraid to go after it. They commonly represent age groups who are eager to make their mark on the world, such as college graduates and young entrepreneurs.

- Personality traits: assertive, idealistic, motivated, action-oriented, headstrong

- Gender: male, or females in masculine roles

- Age group: predominantly 20s and 30s, but may be older

As your experience with the Tarot grows, you may find the court cards represent concepts rather than actual people in your life. For example, the appearance of a knight in your reading may feel more like a message to take charge and move forward with a project. Be open to variable meanings coming from the royal members of the Tarot. Trust your intuition to guide you.

Queens

These personality types are primarily nurturers. Queens represent mothers, as well as women with many social/familial responsibilities. These people are typically in a role of support and service. Because they are responsible for so much, queens tend to be in a position of authority. Others frequently seek the queen's approval or advice. They are caring and generous with their resources in order to help others. They enjoy playing a vital role in the family (either home or work family). They can be fiercely protective and should not be crossed if they feel their value is threatened. They are likely adept at expressing themselves through creative arts like home decorating or fashion. Queens are intuitive and perceptive. This makes them excellent communicators. They negotiate well and are particularly skilled at keeping the peace when disputes arise.

- Personality traits: supportive, shrewd, creative, nurturing, thoughtful, intuitive

- Gender: females, or males in maternal/ nurturing roles

- Age group: predominantly 40+, or mothers of any age and/or women in power at any age

Kings

As you might guess, kings are people in positions of power and influence. These people have amassed great wisdom, and likely have impressive resources at their disposal. Kings are strategists and can be calculating in planning for their future. Kings are innately protective, and they are motivated by keeping their valuables safe. What they consider valuable may range from stockholdings to their family. These people take pride in their accomplishments and are particularly pleased with what they have accumulated in life. Whether their children or their bankroll, kings spend a great deal of time overseeing the wealth obtained in their life. They relish the idea of making things happen by their own skill and might. These people are likely well-respected and others readily take their sage advice. They can be domineering and boastful. However, age and experience often softens these people into having likable and genuinely kind personalities.

- Personality traits: powerful, wise, controlling, successful, fatherly, strategic, influential

- Gender: male, or females in masculine/ paternal roles

- Age group: predominantly 40+, or men/ fathers in positions of respect and authority at any age

THE MAJOR ARCANA

THE FOOL.

THE
FOOL

You're packed, perky, and psyched to jettison off into a new adventure! You feel the power of pure potential all around. The Fool indicates you are compelled to take that first fearless step in a new direction. This card is all about limitless opportunity. The Fool personality is void of all structure, rules, or reason. He is without plan, strategy, or knowledge of destination. The Fool comes frolicking into your readings as a sign of birthing new ideas to pounce upon from a place of excitement and innocent expectation. The Fool beckons you to become like a child. Be a clean slate. Seek out new vistas without preconceived notions or habitual, predetermined thinking.

When contemplating the meaning of The Fool, ask yourself:

Am I following my dreams?

Am I honoring my prime passion?

What would the Fool do in my situation?

What do I value most—my beliefs or my image?

UPRIGHT

Travel • Change • Innocence • Expectation • Spontaneity

REVERSE

Escape • Ignorance • Unprepared • Irresponsibility • Impetuousness

Meaning in a Reading

UPRIGHT	REVERSE

Core Meaning

It's time to move out of the old and into the new you. Whether changing location or changing your world view, you are primed for an easy-going and adventurous transition.

Core Meaning

Poor planning and poor choices in the past have put you in a position to cut your losses and move forward. Learn from past mistakes and take smarter steps into a better future.

Quick-Read Meanings

LOVE

Fall into it! Surrender to your heart. Hop on the roller coaster ride of love with giddy abandon.

Quick-Read Meanings

LOVE

You're blinded by something in the relationship. Get real, get a reality check, and move on.

MONEY

Sheer dumb luck is on your side. Buy a lottery ticket, follow a hunch, or take a chance.

MONEY

Your resources are meager right now, so make the most of them. Invest and spend more wisely.

CAREER

Even if it doesn't make sense, make a bold move in your career. Follow your destiny, not practicality.

CAREER

You've been blind-sided by a terminated job or project. Move through feelings of indecision or loss.

FAMILY

Road trip! Lead your family on a new adventure together. Or it might be time to move out of the nest.

FAMILY

A rash departure from your roots leaves you feeling alone and isolated. Time to find a new support group.

THE FOOL

THE FOOL SAYS...

"Ignore the criticisms of your peers. People may think you're nuts, but at least you're going for the gusto! Ditch your hang-ups, and try a walk on the unconventional side of life. Nothing ventured, nothing gained. Pack only what you need in life (love, faith, wonder) and blaze a new trail!"

THE MAGICIAN.

THE
MAGICIAN

You're in a perfect position to work magic in your life. Maybe you've been waiting for more details to make a decision. The Magician indicates those details coming to light, and you are free to move forward. Feel the power of making choices that honor who you are. The Magician card is a sign you have all the "right stuff." Time, resources, and direction are all aligned for optimal outcomes in your life. The Magician is a powerful card that represents an initiation into a new direction of life. Above all else, The Magician wants you to recognize your full potential, conjure your own magic, and step into your personal power.

When contemplating the meaning of The Magician, ask yourself:

Am I living up to my full potential?

What can I do to achieve more order and stability in my life?

If I had every resource available to me, what could I do to make the world a better place?

How am I using my power?

UPRIGHT

Power • Action • Balance • Potential • Initiation • Resourcefulness

REVERSE

Fear • Lack • Disorder • Ignorance • Imbalance • Insecurity

Meaning in a Reading

UPRIGHT	REVERSE

Core Meaning

It's time to take action. Utilize all the information and resources you have, and make it all work for you. You can do it! Just acknowledge your inner power and potential. You'll be amazed at what you can accomplish!

Core Meaning

A series of events has turned you upside down. This may conjure feelings of fear, imbalance, and a lack of confidence. It may appear you don't have enough resources to solve problems, and this is causing major frustration.

Quick-Read Meanings

LOVE

You're in a place of maturity and accomplishment that makes you a real catch. In relationships, the Magician indicates an equally yoked love.

MONEY

This is a prime time for making investments, taking risks and acting on your instinct. Finances are flourishing, and the promise of prosperity is in the air.

CAREER

You're an ace in your occupation, so go out and shine your light in the professional world. It's time to show off your assets—maybe even brag a little.

FAMILY

The Magician is all about gathering family together and making magical memories that last a lifetime.

Quick-Read Meanings

LOVE

Give love a breather right now. Let emotional unrest settle before you go back into the water and make waves in your love life.

MONEY

Go back and analyze your spending habits, expenses, and investments. You're going to see a trend in your findings. Use your data to get back in the black.

CAREER

Everybody has setbacks in their career. Hold off on taking action until you're in a better position to make a smart decision.

FAMILY

You may be encountering disagreements or confusion within the family right now. Stability can be regained if you keep focused on your ideal home life.

THE MAGICIAN SAYS...

"You've got the power. You may not know it, or maybe you lack confidence, but your potential for greatness ripples just under the surface! Take an inventory of your emotional, physical, mental, and spiritual details. Tally up the good and bad. Put everything together and create something amazing!"

THE MAGICIAN

THE HIGH PRIESTESS.

THE **HIGH PRIESTESS**

Déjà vu, intuition, hunches—oh my! The High Priestess rules the realm of psychic perception. When she shows up in our readings, it's time to tune into intuition and imagination. The High Priestess challenges us to solve problems unconventionally, through our sixth sense. The High Priestess also encourages us to feel our emotions more fully. She asks us to open the floodgates of perception and gain new, other-worldly perspectives.

When contemplating the meaning of The High Priestess, ask yourself:

Am I acting upon or ignoring my intuition?

Am I emotionally connected?

How can I get more comfortable with the unknown?

Do I need to be more patient?

UPRIGHT

Time • Psyche • Shadow • Emotion • Balance • Fertility • Perception

REVERSE

Loss • Mistrust • Impatience • Stagnation

Meaning in a Reading

UPRIGHT	REVERSE

Core Meaning

The High Priestess is all about piercing the darkness and being okay with the unknown. We can pick up a lot of clues for solving life's mysteries by trusting our feelings and intuition. The High Priestess reminds us that all good things come in their own time.

Core Meaning

You're forcing an issue that isn't ready to be revealed. Traditional solutions will not work on the problem you're experiencing. Stop letting small-minded action hold you back from innovative ways of living life.

Quick-Read Meanings

LOVE

There may be something unspoken between you and your partner that is preventing fruitful companionship. Have an open, honest discussion with your loved one.

MONEY

Reevaluate your income and assets—you've been overlooking something that you can take advantage of now.

CAREER

Trust your instinct at work. If you sense something or someone is holding you from progress, you might be right. It's important to be patient and calm in moments of stress.

FAMILY

If you've been thinking about starting a family, this card is a positive sign. This card also encourages balance within the home, and letting conflicts take their course.

Quick-Read Meanings

LOVE

You're torn between two lovers. This could mean toggling between two partners, or maybe struggling between work vs. your mate. Let your emotions lead you to the right choice between two compelling forces.

MONEY

Something of value is missing or has been taken. This may be due to a lack of safeguards. Get legal advice and draw up contracts to protect your assets.

CAREER

Your employer is "flushing out" some of the waste within the organization. If you are part of this clear-out, look at it as an opportunity. A loss means gaining in another area of your professional life.

FAMILY

There is an impasse in your home. Take the emotional high road, and let bygones be bygones. This card is also an invitation to research your genealogy.

THE HIGH PRIESTESS

 ## THE HIGH PRIESTESS SAYS...

"Let go! Put your inner control freak to rest. Sometimes the best action is inaction. Remember, life is a perfect mystery, and it is unfolding in perfect ways. As babies, we are born with super-keen powers of perception. Trust in these powers; they are still with you."

THE
EMPRESS

Congratulations! You're expecting! The Empress is an announcement for new birth in your life. This doesn't necessarily mean a new baby. It could be the birth of a new idea or opportunity. The Empress card is an icon for new creations. She indicates we are in line to receive the fruits of our labor. The Empress also represents motherhood and feminine influence. She reminds us to nurture and protect that which is helpless or in need of nurturing or support. This could be as simple as giving your child a gesture of comfort, or as grand as becoming an activist for global preservation.

When contemplating the meaning of The Empress, ask yourself:

How can I nurture myself and others more?

What are my feelings about motherhood?

What can I do to assist a new birth in my life?

How can I connect with Mother Nature in a profound way?

UPRIGHT

Birth • Abundance • Protection • Motherhood • Creativity • Femininity

REVERSE

Neglect • Rejection • Resistance • Empty promises • Counterproductive

Meaning in a Reading

UPRIGHT	REVERSE

UPRIGHT

Core Meaning

The Empress is perfectly comfortable with her responsibilities as a caregiver, guardian, and ruler. She is a role model, and she beckons us to embrace the role of protecting the sanctity of life in this world.

Quick-Read Meanings

LOVE

This is a blossoming and fruitful time for you and your partner. It may also be a time to contemplate starting a new family, or a new creative venture with your mate.

MONEY

You have worked hard on your financial situation. You've been saving, or planning for better monetary return. Now you're going to see the pay-off.

CAREER

This is a prime time to start new projects and take on new responsibility at work. You're going to experience heightened creativity. Act on your ideas with authority and confidence.

FAMILY

Expect a new addition to your family. It could be a baby, or maybe even a new puppy. It might even signal the "ok" to build a new addition on your family home.

REVERSE

Core Meaning

It's confounding! You've put in the time and made the effort, but it seems your hard work isn't paying off. There are some blockages you need to clear out before you see the results you want.

Quick-Read Meanings

LOVE

Look around you! There is so much to love and cherish, but you're not paying attention. You may also be ignoring the affections of an admirer.

MONEY

Your financial flow feels like it's running upstream. No amount of brute force is going to switch those streams. The best course of action is to give thanks for what you have, and wait out the financial drought.

CAREER

You might be "in your head" too much at work, and overcomplicating things. Consider employing a simple, basic, tried-and-true approach.

FAMILY

You may be experiencing "empty nest" syndrome right now. Perhaps a child has moved out of the home, or the hope of familial achievement was not fulfilled. The sense of emptiness will pass.

THE EMPRESS SAYS...

"There is a season for all things. I'm a reminder that promise and bounty is available to you even when everything appears bleak and barren. Nurture yourself and others by giving thanks for blessings. Expect renewal and love to bloom in your life."

THE EMPRESS

THE
EMPEROR

The Emperor is the male counterpart to The Empress. The Emperor represents man's place in the world, and his role as a leader. Pulling this card means you need to seat yourself in the throne of leadership. The Emperor does not doubt his authority, and expects the same from you. This confidence comes from years of practice being a ruler. Either you have the experience to be an effective leader, or you need to respect someone who does. It's time to step up and believe in yourself and your ability to take charge. The Emperor is a just and capable ruler. He reminds us to respect our elders and leaders.

When contemplating the meaning of The Emperor, ask yourself:

How do I feel about fatherhood?

Am I a good leader? How can I be better?

Should I consult an elder or expert about something?

Do I respect authority figures?

Can I delegate? Or am I too controlling?

UPRIGHT

Power • Fairness • Authority • Masculinity

REVERSE

Cold • Inflexible • Seriousness • Lack of control

Meaning in a Reading

UPRIGHT	REVERSE

Core Meaning

You have seen and experienced a lot in your life. You have enough perspective to give instructions and lead a group. Be fair, and employ wisdom. The Emperor may also represent a strong father-figure who is extending advice worth taking.

Core Meaning

Although you may have experienced some success as a leader, now it feels like the job is weighing you down. The weight of responsibility is becoming overwhelming. You've become hardened and inflexible in your attitude toward life.

Quick-Read Meanings

LOVE

We all play our roles in partnership, but watch you're not too overbearing or bossy with your mate. Pay attention to leadership roles in your relationship.

MONEY

It's time to call in an expert. Seek a seasoned accountant or financial advisor for advice about your monetary situation.

CAREER

When you are called to be a leader in your career, treat the position with respect. It's also time to delegate and supervise more.

FAMILY

The upright Emperor is all about father-figures. It's time for the dad in your life to embrace the role of fatherhood, and perhaps re-evaluate his role in the family.

Quick-Read Meanings

LOVE

You're taking it all too seriously. Whether you are seeking love (and not finding it), or in a relationship—try being less intense about your attitude toward love.

MONEY

Your financial foundation seems turned upside-down. Now is the time to grow some thick skin. Collect the debts owed to you. Also consider diversifying. Strategize to put more than one stream of income in place.

CAREER

You're dealing with a glass ceiling in your career. It appears there is no chance for promotion or advancement. You're going to have to move around this impasse if you want to move up on the ladder.

FAMILY

The balance of power in the family is unequal. Discipline is lacking. This causes confusion, resentment, and hard feelings. Family members need to be clear about what is expected of them.

THE EMPEROR

 THE EMPEROR SAYS...

"I am a strong ruler with complete control over my kingdom. When you see me in a reading, you must remember that being a ruler isn't the same as being a cold-hearted tyrant. Listen to advice from those who know more than you. Rule your realm with maturity, fairness, and balance."

THE HIEROPHANT.

THE
HIEROPHANT

The word *hierophant* means "holy" in ancient Greek. The Hierophant is a priest, counselor, teacher, or holy person who serves as a go-between for mankind and god/spirit. Consequently, this card deals with religious and spiritual themes. The Hierophant is revealed when we need to protect our faith, seek spiritual guidance, or rededicate ourselves to some form of religious worship. This card also stands for tradition, ceremony, and spiritual law. In its simplest translation, The Hierophant is a sign of spiritual blessing.

When contemplating the meaning of The Hierophant, ask yourself:

How healthy is my faith?

Should I incorporate more tradition in my life?

What are my views about religion and religious figures?

Am I equally balanced between physical and spiritual?

UPRIGHT

Holy • Sacred • Ceremony • Guidance • Tradition • Spirituality

REVERSE

Disgrace • Hypocrisy • Backsliding • Disobedience • Disillusioned • Untraditional

Meaning in a Reading

UPRIGHT	REVERSE

Core Meaning

It's time to seek spiritual guidance in your life. The Hierophant may be a sign of marriage, communion, or re-devotion of faith. This card signifies a public show of union, faith, or devotion.

Core Meaning

You may be dealing with a crisis in faith. Maybe you've been let down by people or an institution in which you put your trust. The reversed Hierophant indicates a fall from grace.

Quick-Read Meanings

LOVE

This card indicates a formal declaration of love. This could suggest approaching a father-figure for a blessing in marriage, or it could mean a traditional ceremony to publicly declare love of any kind (including love of god).

MONEY

Your focus on money is out of proportion. Moderation and balance are key in your financial outlook. Also consider giving to a charity or spiritual organization of your preference.

CAREER

Be mindful of people in authority, and do your best to comply with their rules and expectations.

FAMILY

If tensions are high in your home, it may be time to seek family counseling or guidance. Focus on family values and tradition.

Quick-Read Meanings

LOVE

You or your partner may feel distracted and withdraw affections from one another. Talk honestly about these feelings and get them out in the open.

MONEY

You can't count on charity to help you out of a financial bind. Your current lack is due to your own negligence. Stop blaming others for your shortcomings. Stop relying on others to bail you out.

CAREER

The traditional career track isn't working for you. Consider taking an unconventional approach to work, especially if you are of retirement age.

FAMILY

It's time to incorporate ceremony, tradition, and faith into the family. This could be as simple as establishing a traditional weekly game night with the whole family. Or try regular visits to your place of worship.

THE HIEROPHANT

THE HIEROPHANT SAYS...

"As a liaison between man and god, I have specialized skills in communicating common ideas in spiritual ways. Seek guidance using your belief and faith. Often, belief in the spiritual world is a catalyst for moving mountains in the physical world."

THE LOVERS.

THE
LOVERS

Yes, The Lovers card is an absolute sign of love, but there's more to it than just hearts and cupids. The card expresses a lot of symbolism related to health, healing, balance, and feeling natural. The Lovers card encourages healthy partnerships, physical well-being, and finding ways to be our best selves. It also deals with generosity, compassion, and creative expression. Trust is a big keyword for The Lovers card. In a reading, this card encourages honesty and transparency when dealing with others and ourselves.

When contemplating the meaning of The Lovers, ask yourself:

Am I being truthful with myself and others?

Am I too self-seeking and selfish?

How is vulnerability a strength?

Do I believe in the full power of love?

UPRIGHT

Love • Health • Harmony • Blessing • Unification

REVERSE

Loss • Shame • Illusion • Hedonism • Temptation

Meaning in a Reading

UPRIGHT	REVERSE

Core Meaning

This is a time of tremendous growth for you. Expect to receive love, healing, and joy. New partnerships are likely—particularly the kind that promote more balance in your life. Keep your focus on truth and goodness.

Core Meaning

Hedonism is succumbing to primal urges and wanting only what feels good now—no matter the consequences. The Lovers in reverse is a reminder of this potential within all of us.

Quick-Read Meanings

LOVE

Expect to meet a mate who will treat you as an equal. Your existing relationships will be rekindled. Growth, harmony, and understanding is promised in partnerships. Do not be too impulsive, and keep your libido in check.

MONEY

You will gain a deep understanding of give-and-take. The more you give with a loving heart, the more you will receive.

CAREER

Be mindful of different gender and cultural issues at work. There is a delicate balance among your peers. You will be amazed at how easy and agreeable the workplace will become.

FAMILY

If a misunderstanding caused a rift with a family member, now is the perfect time to heal it. Family is receptive to you, and forgiveness is at hand.

Quick-Read Meanings

LOVE

You may be experiencing powerful desires and urges. An infatuation of some sort has blinded you from priorities. Seek counsel from a mentor or spiritual guide in order to gain balance and perspective.

MONEY

You took some bad financial advice, and now you're experiencing the fall-out from that misguidance. Become transparent and prepare for a fresh start.

CAREER

You have suddenly found yourself exposed at work. Perhaps you've been covering for someone, or masking your own performance. Come clean and be honest.

FAMILY

A family misunderstanding worsens because petty details are clouding the issue. Give your family members some time to regroup. Revisit the issue with candor and unemotional honesty.

THE LOVERS

THE LOVERS SAY...

"As Lovers, we can tell you 50/50 partnerships work best. This kind of harmony comes from tolerance, understanding, and compassion. Do not allow pettiness or selfishness to rule your relationships. Love is a dance in which both partners step backward and forward in equal measure."

THE
CHARIOT

Action, decision, drive, and stamina. These are themes of the Chariot, and they are expressed in terms of progress and navigation. The Chariot is about planning our course to win a victory. We must employ level-headed strategy to get to our destination. The Chariot encourages us to stay focused and drive on to our goals without fear of the unknown. Confidence, intellect, and self-control wins the battle. At its simplest, The Chariot card is a sign of travel, relocation, and/or transportation.

When contemplating the meaning of The Chariot, ask yourself:

What drives me? Why?

What kind of distractions keep me from my goals?

What am I trying to control, and why?

Can I take a different approach to reaching my goals?

UPRIGHT

Travel • Victory • Confidence • Motivation • Accomplishment

REVERSE

Denial • Setback • Unstable • Unrealistic

Meaning in a Reading

UPRIGHT	REVERSE

Core Meaning

Take charge! The Chariot asks you to recall past accomplishments and reach for the stars. Plan for success. Educate yourself on how to go from point A to B in order to reach your goals.

Core Meaning

You're stalled, feeling flat, and stuck. Emotional issues are pulling you down, and you're unclear about what you should do about it. The Chariot is a powerful card of force and drive. You won't be sluggish for long.

Quick-Read Meanings

LOVE

To experience a rock-solid relationship, you must temper overemotional reactions. Be even-minded, fair, and calm when dealing with your partner.

MONEY

Strong reliance upon community or a support group has led you to higher financial ground. Pay it forward.

CAREER

Move forward with a plan or strategy you developed to further your career. Double check your facts and make a contingency plan because there's no backing out once you make your move.

FAMILY

There's nothing wrong with having a productive, active family life, but make sure your family has a proper balance of work and play.

Quick-Read Meanings

LOVE

There is a switch in roles between you and your partner. You have a choice to go with the flow, or fight against change. You may save the relationship some battle scars if you work in tandem with your partner.

MONEY

It's time for a change. Constantly using the same approach about your financial planning is going to get you stuck. Make educated choices and navigate your money with confidence. Look abroad for funding.

CAREER

Don't let setbacks in your career frustrate you. This is the perfect time to go back to school or learn more about your industry through independent study.

FAMILY

Responsibilities are shirked, and there is a lack of teamwork within the household. Take initiative, and family members will follow your lead.

THE CHARIOT

THE CHARIOT SAYS ...

"Set your mind, clear your path. You have loads of support to get you where you need to go. Nothing can deter you from your goal. You have a lot riding on your success, but you must not let this intimidate you. Do not let your attention be divided."

STRENGTH

In most societies, the term *strength* is attributed to masculinity, yet this card features a woman. Feminine energy is not about brute force, and neither is the Strength card. This card is about balancing our animal nature and our higher nature. It's about using compassion to tame the wild, unruly elements within ourselves and our environment. The card reminds us that peace, love, and staying calm in a crisis are the best ways to express strength. The Strength card may also represent family pets as well as health and balance.

When contemplating the meaning of Strength, ask yourself:

How might I expand my definition of strength?

How can I maximize power through self-love and compassion?

What are some ways I can temper my anger?

How can I purify myself and be at peace with the chaos around me?

UPRIGHT

Preparation • Facing fears • Self-control • Battle of will

REVERSE

Struggle • Overwhelmed • Inconsistency • Abuse of power

Meaning in a Reading

UPRIGHT	REVERSE

Core Meaning

You are prepared to face great challenges. You have mastered yourself, your additions and dependencies. This allows you to reveal your best strengths. Poise, grace, and a sense of self-worth are the strongest influences when dealing with challenges.

Core Meaning

You're dealing with power-plays and struggling for dominance. The irony is, the more you try to gain control by force, the more powerless you become. Eventually, you're going to have to surrender, and take a different approach to manage conflict.

Quick-Read Meanings

LOVE

You're struggling with a willful faction within your relationship. Don't engage in arguments. Instead, be patient and understanding. Approach the situation with serenity.

MONEY

You sense a flare-up in your finances, and it has you worried. Be detached and unemotional about the situation. You may discover there is no need for worry.

CAREER

Part of you wants to toss all responsibilities to the side and take a wild risk in your career. Temper this impulse with preparation and careful thought.

FAMILY

There's an emotional flood in your family life. The only way to keep control is to apply a strong and steady stream of understanding, love, and compassion to the situation.

Quick-Read Meanings

LOVE

There is a big disagreement or argument. Your side is correct, but your partner isn't listening or seeing your point. Removing yourself from the conflict might be your only recourse.

MONEY

Frivolous spending, gambling, and cheating will catch up with you. Beware of "easy money" because it always comes with strings attached.

CAREER

A situation or a boss is putting unreasonable demands upon you. Your instinct is to bite back at your boss, but resist this urge. Keep calm, and carry on.

FAMILY

The matriarch in your family is either missing or weakened. This causes overwhelming burdens, grief, and imbalance. Find ways to help mom out, remember her, honor her.

STRENGTH

 STRENGTH SAYS...

"Life can be a roaring, raging beast. At every turn, the world seems ready to take a bite out of us. Employ empathy, compassion, and patience with yourself and others. Rely on your values and integrity to restore your faith in others. Do these things consistently and do not allow doubt to invade your heart."

THE
HERMIT

The term *hermit* is Greek for "in the desert." The hermit label was popularly used for people who led a monastic life in early Christianity. The Hermit devotes his life to religious/spiritual study. He purposefully removes himself from all worldly influences to be one with god. In a reading, The Hermit illustrates a need to turn away from the world and go within for answers. The Hermit signals a time of quietude, introspection, and deep thought.

When contemplating the meaning of The Hermit, ask yourself:

Am I able to get quiet, be still, and simply "be"?

How can I carve out some "me" time or meditate once a day to get centered?

What is my level of awareness in this moment?

Is it time to re-devote myself to religious studies?

UPRIGHT

Prayer • Isolation • Introspection • Contemplation • Enlightenment

REVERSE

Edgy • Cold • Cerebral • Withdrawn

Meaning in a Reading

UPRIGHT	REVERSE

Core Meaning

The Hermit encourages you to get untangled from petty, superficial distractions. Embark on a spiritual journey, or spend time contemplating life in silence. Daily meditations in a quiet place can work wonders for your inner peace and tranquility.

Core Meaning

You have lost connection to your heart, your emotions, or your faith. This card often signals a depression so deep, you can't see your way out. Feelings of withdrawal, reclusiveness, and being an outcast intensify loneliness and depression.

Quick-Read Meanings

LOVE

There's a difference between being alone and feeling lonely. Be okay with being alone. There is no true love with a partner unless you love yourself first.

Quick-Read Meanings

LOVE

A sign of rejection or failed relationships. Feelings of bitterness and hatefulness toward the idea of love. Use this alone time to improve yourself for the sake of loving yourself.

MONEY

Your accounts are frozen, but don't despair. A lull in financial activity will allow you to regroup and recover, putting you in a better position in the future.

MONEY

You're feeling imprisoned due to mindless money-making decisions. Try unconventional measures to reverse your financial paralysis.

CAREER

You've got a bright idea nobody else seems to understand. Thomas Edison failed hundreds of times, but kept believing in his bright idea. The Hermit recommends you do the same.

CAREER

The reversed Hermit often represents unemployment or a void in vocation. Becoming hardened and cold will only worsen your prospects.

FAMILY

Your family may be supportive, but they might also be holding you back. Perhaps it's time to become more independent and make your own way.

FAMILY

Perhaps you've been outcast from your family or support group. If you're a natural lone-wolf, the isolation will serve you well. Otherwise, look within to find your unique brilliance.

THE HERMIT SAYS...

"It's wise to seek advice, but in the end you only have yourself to live with, so make choices according to your own needs. Going your own way requires a strong belief in yourself and your ideas. Every step you take to honor your unique self is a step to freedom and enlightenment."

THE HERMIT

WHEEL OF FORTUNE.

WHEEL OF FORTUNE

When pulling The Wheel of Fortune, it's important to identify what is at the hub of your life. Know what keeps you focused. Be clear about your top-priorities. Why? Because The Wheel of Fortune represents unpredictable and sometimes turbulent events happening in your life. Fortune can be cruel or kind. In either case, it's vital to have a fixed center of gravity while the world spins around you. No matter what fate throws your way, you must not let it distract you from your core values.

When contemplating the meaning of Wheel of Fortune ask yourself:

Do I feel lucky? Why?

Is it possible to change my luck and fortune?

How do I handle change?

Do I have a backup or a contingency plan?

What are the consequences of my thoughts and actions?

UPRIGHT

Luck • Chance • Cycles • Change • Destiny

REVERSE

Awareness • Intellect • Discernment • Foundations

Meaning in a Reading

UPRIGHT	REVERSE

Core Meaning

This card signals a change in fortune (good or bad), and it often comes in unpredictable ways. The Wheel of Fortune is also symbolic of consequence. What comes up, must come down.

Core Meaning

The Wheel of Fortune reversed encourages full-disclosure before taking action. Do the research. Prepare the way. Look before you leap. There is a consequence for every action.

Quick-Read Meanings

LOVE

Overly stimulated, and overly distracted—this card indicates a dizzying array of activity in your love life. You may also feel as though love is taking you for a ride.

MONEY

Gambling and games of chance might offer you a lucky break in your finances. Just know that you can't bank on luck all the time.

CAREER

You are dealing with an unstable work environment. You may be tempted to take a shot at a different position to avoid discomfort or insecurity. Wait out the fear—stability will return.

FAMILY

Does your family work for a common goal? If so, then you need not worry about life throwing your family off-kilter. If not, then you may experience a shaky foundation. Changes such as relocations or new additions to the family may be nigh.

Quick-Read Meanings

LOVE

Something in your past has been dredged back up into your present. In order to safeguard your future, you're going to have to address the issue with tact and smart diplomacy.

MONEY

Ground yourself in tried-and-true methods of making money. Don't try new tricks.

CAREER

There's nothing wrong with dreaming big, but your head has been in the clouds for too long. Now is the time to form your imaginings into reality.

FAMILY

Reaffirm rock-solid values within the home. Don't let bad behavior slide. If you are the head of the household, be aware the whole family models, compares, and mimics your behavior.

WHEEL OF FORTUNE SAYS ...

"If unpredictability makes you nervous, try developing a sense of humor and going with the flow. Life is meant to be enjoyed. Even the downturns can offer beauty and opportunity. If you thrive on change, be sure you have a sound center of gravity. Don't allow the wild revolutions of life to shake you off balance."

WHEEL OF FORTUNE

41

JUSTICE

Logically, the Justice card stands for truth, relying on facts, and gathering details in order to form an educated decision. In a reading, Justice points to matters of law. Legal action, lawsuits, and contracts are all under this heading. Internally, this card encourages self-honesty, moderation, and balancing our life-affairs. Be fair. Be prudent. Stay objective.

When contemplating the meaning of Justice, ask yourself:

Should I take legal action?

Am I ignoring the problem? Why?

How can justice be served?

Am I impartial? Or is my bias holding back progress?

How can I honor the truth in this situation?

UPRIGHT

Truth • Judgment • Legalities • Impartiality

REVERSE

Ignorance • Assumption • Immaturity • Misinformation • Lack of conviction

Meaning in a Reading

UPRIGHT	REVERSE

Core Meaning

A legal situation is in process, pending, or upcoming. Justice will be served. Your responsibility is to be transparent, honest, and level-headed in the situation.

Core Meaning

Even the best intended action becomes an epic fail if you can't follow through with a plan. Whatever the case, reversed Justice advises you to regain stable footing, regroup, and employ a well-informed strategy.

Quick-Read Meanings

LOVE

50/50 is the rule in your partnerships. You may have experienced a tipping of the scales in the past, but you will be shown how to maintain balance in love now.

MONEY

Be cautious and thorough before signing contracts or making agreements concerning your financial future.

CAREER

Consider going to a professional employment agency to assist with career placement. Legal action may be necessary to make progress on the work front.

FAMILY

Establish clear expectations about household chores/policies. Custody suits and/or domestic disputes will come to a head. Truth will be served in these matters.

Quick-Read Meanings

LOVE

You've been wronged, and have an urge to retaliate or take revenge. Retribution is ill-advised. Call on professional help or get a strong friend to assist you in solving the conflict.

MONEY

Take a second look at what you value. Digging for more information will save you in the long run.

CAREER

Avoid taking your anger or frustration out on others at the workplace. Consider going back to school or get more training. This will justify your recognition and promotion.

FAMILY

You're ignoring some obvious signs in the family to avoid confrontation. The more you refuse to see the truth, the more the problem will grow.

JUSTICE SAYS...

"It's been said justice is blind. Do not allow favoritism, money, or power to tarnish the facts at hand. Moreover, be level-headed and get all the facts before you proceed. Make sure you can commit to your choices, and allow fairness to guide your way."

JUSTICE

THE HANGED MAN

The Hanged Man represents surrender. We encounter this card typically after wrestling for a solution, but we get strung up by the consequences anyway. In fact, when we fight harder, we only succeed in working ourselves into knots. Now we must either admit defeat, or surrender to the situation. Suspend the urge to struggle. Inaction will give you a breather, and this will give you space to gain clarity for a better solution. The Hanged Man also suggests accepting our punishment with serenity if we have knowingly committed a wrongdoing.

When contemplating the meaning of The Hanged Man, ask yourself:

What would happen if I simply surrendered?

What if being at a crossroads is a positive thing?

What kind of bright ideas can I present to the world?

How is struggle or denial helping me?

UPRIGHT

Inaction • Revelation • Getting caught • Accepting responsibility

REVERSE

Levity • Exoneration • Understanding • Determination

Meaning in a Reading

UPRIGHT	REVERSE

Core Meaning

You can no longer struggle to get out of a situation. Being at the crossroads might feel paralyzing, but if you surrender to the way things are, a solution will come at the perfect time.

Core Meaning

You grappled with some tough issues, but now the weight of responsibility has been lifted from you and you are free. Now that you are free to move on, which direction will you take at the crossroads of life?

Quick-Read Meanings

LOVE

Your hands are tied in a relationship. Be honest with your mate, and face the music.

MONEY

Your finances are tied up right now, but you've got a brilliant money-making idea under your hat. Now is the time to put that idea into play.

CAREER

Take criticism at work with serious consideration. Examining this will prompt you to branch into other work, or make the most of the work you have.

FAMILY

Just because some things aren't working out doesn't mean you have to hang the whole plan. Take a break from the issue and focus on the family ideals you aimed for in the first place.

Quick-Read Meanings

LOVE

There is no need to prove yourself right, because your partner already knows he/she is wrong. Give your partner time to come around.

MONEY

Things might be tight, but stand your ground and hang tough. Relief is coming.

CAREER

It might feel like you're tip-toeing around the office due to a stressful atmosphere. Keep your head clear, and your nose to the grindstone.

FAMILY

There is a family member who refuses to conform or comply with the rules. Being rigid only aggravates the situation. Find a tactic that will allow freedom within reason.

THE HANGED MAN SAYS...

"Nobody likes to get caught doing something wrong, but it happens to all of us. If you can bear the consequences with humility, the payment for misdoings will be lenient, and your lessons will be long-lasting. Surrendering to the inevitable will provide you with a remarkable sense of relief."

DEATH

The idea of death can be a scary thing, and seeing it in a spread can be dubious at best. Although it sometimes indicates physical death, a more likely interpretation deals with the end of a particular phase in life. Change, metamorphosis, and transition are the watchwords for the Death card. This card also illustrates the importance of dying to our sinful nature. It encourages setting aside corporeal fixations like greed, lust, and addiction in order to live free. At its simplest, the Death card indicates a swift change in life that forces a loss to make room for gain. The biggest lesson Death offers is to take nothing for granted.

When contemplating the meaning of Death, ask yourself:

How will my life be different if I accept change rather than resist it?

How can I slow down, and get back to basics?

How can I take a more effective stand for my beliefs?

What if every ending meant a new beginning?

UPRIGHT

Ending • Transition • Impermanence • Inevitability

REVERSE

Rigid • Resistance • Taking a stand • Back to basics

Meaning in a Reading

UPRIGHT	REVERSE

Core Meaning

Our only guarantee in life is change. Endings are inevitable. The trick is to lay ourselves bare to loss. Doing so will make transitions easier, and allow new opportunities to enter our lives.

Core Meaning

It's going to feel like the whole world is railing against your efforts to stand for your beliefs. Your surroundings are moving and transitioning so fast it's going to be hard to stay resolute in the midst of the chaos. Keep your footing.

Quick-Read Meanings

LOVE

You or your loved one may be struggling with some issues that are bigger than you're able to handle. It's time to make a hard decision whether to stay or leave the relationship.

MONEY

Your relationship with money is unhealthy. Explore other sources of value that do not diminish, like love or spiritual wealth.

CAREER

Cut backs, lay-offs, and downsizing may affect your career. Suppress the urge to react or respond with fear. A door closing means a window opening.

FAMILY

A harsh reality within the family has left you feeling vulnerable and empty. Move forward. The awkwardness will abate in time. Be patient.

Quick-Read Meanings

LOVE

Consider taking a break in the relationship. You have to figure out who you are and what you need before the relationship can go further.

MONEY

Others have ulterior motives that might not be in your best interest. Rely on your own resources and instincts before trusting your finances to others.

CAREER

It's time to get back to basics. A simple work ethic, basic skills, and common sense are the elements for success.

FAMILY

You had an ideal, but no one else is following your leadership. Stand your ground. Others will see your passion, and eventually come around.

 ## DEATH SAYS...

"Change is inevitable. You can either rail against the idea of death and endings, or you can move with these transitions. The stance you take can make all the difference between peace or conflict in your life. You make the choice."

TEMPERANCE

Temperance is moderation in action. This card is about maintaining a healthy lifestyle, showing restraint concerning excess, and working toward harmony. This card also encourages moderation in our environment. Mindfulness about conservation, rehabilitation, and global healing are at the forefront. The Temperance card encourages cleansing, purification, and taking a holistic approach to life. The card reflects the vital balance of giving and receiving. There is an energetic exchange in every aspect of life. The Temperance card asks us to discover a happy medium in life's daily exchanges.

When contemplating the meaning of Temperance, ask yourself:

How can I more easily go with the flow?

How can I establish moderation and balance in my life?

How can I make a positive global impact?

Should I be more health conscious?

UPRIGHT

Healing • Harmony • Moderation • Environment • Creative expression

REVERSE

Waste • Excess • Selfish • Overwhelmed • Inconsideration

48

Meaning in a Reading

UPRIGHT	REVERSE

Core Meaning

Turn away from selfish behavior and cease living in isolation. Step out and consider the needs of others. Bring harmony and healing to your family. Larger actions can be made to bring value to your neighborhood. Contribute to global sustainability and conservation.

Core Meaning

There is no moderation, no balance, and emotional upheaval from instability. This off-kilter state prompts overwhelming feelings, which often cause withdrawal and disconnection from the world.

Quick-Read Meanings

LOVE

Employ more creativity in your relationship. Consider going on a healing retreat or visiting a spa with your partner. Try volunteering or building a garden together.

MONEY

You're in a great position to even out your finances. Execute moderation, smart spending, and balanced solutions.

CAREER

You need to find equilibrium between two worlds. Sacrificing prestige or status at work for quality of life will pay off.

FAMILY

A healing has or will soon take place within the family. Promote wholesomeness and renewal by enjoying simple activities like nature walks, watching sunsets, or teaching your kids to fish.

Quick-Read Meanings

LOVE

Putting your own needs before those of your partner has pushed your mate away. Ironically, selfishness comes from a lack of self-love. Nurture yourself in healthy ways.

MONEY

Try not to attach your self-worth to your monetary status. Regain stability by curtailing wasteful spending.

CAREER

Disengage from frustration by helping others. Philanthropy and volunteerism will lead to bright ideas and a better future.

FAMILY

Either your generosity is being taken advantage of, or you are shunning help from others. Resist the temptation to resent those who abuse your kindness. Accept help if it's offered.

TEMPERANCE

TEMPERANCE SAYS...

"The universe operates on balance. Rather than going to extreme swings of the pendulum, make efforts to employ moderate movements in your life. Steady, harmonious choices for positive change reap remarkable benefits."

THE
DEVIL

Negative influences are prohibiting you from living a full, free, happy life. It could be a slight irritation working on your nerves—the kind that grows when left unchecked. It could be a major burden like addiction. Anger, hate, or bitterness are at the forefront of your emotions. The Devil is anything that takes control and puts you into emotional bondage. Abuse, imbalance, and struggles with your animal nature are all issues The Devil stirs up in a reading. When this card appears, your prime question and answer is about control. Are you in control? Or is adversity controlling you?

When contemplating the meaning of The Devil, ask yourself:

Do I always need control? Why?

How often does anger, hate, or resentment get the best of me? Why?

What does it mean to be vulnerable? Is it a weakness or a strength?

What can I do to resist temptation?

UPRIGHT

Sin • Abuse • Control • Imbalance

REVERSE

Relief • Humility • Improvement • Realizations • Vulnerability

Meaning in a Reading

UPRIGHT	REVERSE

Core Meaning

The only power The Devil has is the ability to delude you into thinking you are powerless. This card urges you to take a hard look at what holds you back, and what makes you feel weak or ineffective.

Core Meaning

Trials and tribulations experienced in the past give you unique perspective and realizations. You now know that vulnerability and humility do not equate to weakness. Instead, these are vital keys for a healthy, balanced life.

Quick-Read Meanings

LOVE

Some sort of abuse is going on in your relationship. Feelings of shame, guilt, and worthlessness are crippling. Break the chains.

MONEY

Being a slave to money or materialism has you struggling for balance. Time to reprioritize.

CAREER

You're dealing with a tyrant boss. It could be a superior, or the taskmaster could be you. Resist the urge to react with anger.

FAMILY

Consider letting your family members be who they are. Demands and expectations are unreasonable. The effects are causing resentment and bitterness.

Quick-Read Meanings

LOVE

It's been a rocky road, but your relationship is finally starting to stabilize. The less defensive and reactive you are, the more improvements you'll see.

MONEY

Bad financial moves have left you weary. Don't overcompensate for shortcomings, and don't let setbacks paralyze you with fear.

CAREER

Either you recently escaped from a bad job, or you need to consider breaking away from one. Better opportunities are on the horizon.

FAMILY

After many sleepless nights seized with fear and worry, you experience relief. Concern for a loved one abates because a long-term solution is now surfacing.

THE DEVIL

 ## THE DEVIL SAYS...

"In this day and age, it's easy to be distracted away from morals, values, and faith. The moment you move away from virtue, you become a victim. Being lost is nothing more than letting outside influences have control over you. Choose your power, don't let it choose you."

THE TOWER.

THE
TOWER

You've been blind-sided. A sudden shock to your system has rocked your world, and left you reeling. To add insult to injury, the signs were there—you just chose not to see them. Your focus was on building something bigger and better. There's nothing wrong with wanting more, and focusing your efforts to get it. However, The Tower hints your focus was misinformed and obsessive, and you let other areas of your life suffer from neglect. The upheaval you're experiencing is the universe's way of re-establishing a healthy balance. Use this to adjust your focus and pay attention to areas in your life you've ignored.

When contemplating the meaning of The Tower, ask yourself:

Where is the silver lining in this problem?

Am I overreacting to the situation?

How can I get creative and prosper from this situation?

Am I lying to myself? Why?

UPRIGHT

Shock • Calamity • Upheaval • Inspiration

REVERSE

Force • Denial • Backward • Bailing out • Overreacting

Meaning in a Reading

UPRIGHT	REVERSE

Core Meaning

You've suffered a traumatic setback, but it might not be as bad as you think. Part of the trauma is due to the unexpected shock of the news. Whatever you do, don't react to the situation. When fate strikes out of nowhere, it's usually followed with a golden opportunity.

Core Meaning

You have no choice but to make a decision. Denial and giving up aren't going to make the situation any better. Get clear about what to do, and take cool-headed action.

Quick-Read Meanings

LOVE

All of a sudden, plans fell through, phone calls stopped coming, or somebody went cold fish in the relationship. Resist the urge to pursue. Instead, move forward and rebuild.

MONEY

The best action to take in recent financial distress is no action at all.

CAREER

A business partnership suddenly dissolved, leaving you scrambling to restructure your work. This restructuring is going to give you a major stroke of inspiration.

FAMILY

A recent upheaval has your family up in arms. The signs were there, but they were ignored beneath an icy silence. Open up dialogue and start rebuilding your family relations.

Quick-Read Meanings

LOVE

If you're getting the cold shoulder, it's because you overreacted to something your partner did. Look within and figure out what's at the root of your strong feelings.

MONEY

Do the opposite of what you've been doing and get back in the black.

CAREER

You made a stand and agreed to a big commitment. You tried hard to keep your promises and make things work, but this path isn't working for you.

FAMILY

The family member who takes care of everything wants to bail out because the pressure is too much. Apologize and help with responsibilities. If it's you, find healthy ways to help your family understand your value.

THE TOWER

 ## THE TOWER SAYS...

"Don't obsess or build on an illusion. If you do, don't be surprised when your fantasies come crashing down around you. Be smart, think things through. Build on a practical plan that is time-tested and based on integrity."

THE
STAR

Finally, after a term of challenges and difficulties you are seeing the light at the end of the tunnel. Expect important communications about new opportunities and directions. You learned many lessons about giving and receiving. This puts you in a place of power. You have clarity about your path, and confidence in yourself. Bright ideas are forthcoming. You are in a remarkable place of clarity and creativity. Inspiration, optimism, and renewed energy are prime themes in your life right now.

When contemplating the meaning of The Star, ask yourself:

Do I feel worthy of the good that comes to me?

How can I be more comfortable in my own skin?

How can I cleanse my emotions and experience renewal?

Am I aware of my energy and how I expend it?

UPRIGHT

Renewal • Clarity • Direction • Creativity

REVERSE

Burdens • Confusion • Exhaustion • Wastefulness

Meaning in a Reading

UPRIGHT	REVERSE

Core Meaning

You traveled long and hard to earn this break. Give yourself permission to enjoy a period of satisfaction, peace, and serenity. Rejoice in renewed health, purification, and a burst of creative energy.

Core Meaning

You are pouring out all of your resources and saving nothing for reserves. You may be unsure which direction to take. You need to conserve your energy, otherwise your health will pay the price.

Quick-Read Meanings

LOVE

Feeling starry-eyed about a potential love connection? Odds are in your favor.

MONEY

The stars are in your favor for financial gains. Consider investing in renewable resources and environmentally conscious companies.

CAREER

If you take a new position it will be rewarding, but you'll need to pour all your energy and resources into it at first. Make sure you're up to the challenge.

FAMILY

A heart-to-heart with family gives you clarity and insight. Old hurts will heal after an emotional cleansing.

Quick-Read Meanings

LOVE

You might be wasting time trying to connect with someone. Consider other potential partners who are more receptive to your efforts.

MONEY

There is a massive leak in your finances somewhere on the books. Find it, and plug it up before more money goes down the drain.

CAREER

You've been presented with several opportunities. Take time to meditate on each one, and make your best choice.

FAMILY

Responsibilities in the home have you feeling tired and in dire need of a break. Consider taking some time away from the family for yourself.

THE STAR

THE STAR SAYS...

"It's likely you've been wandering around in an emotional desert for awhile, but wander no more. Get ready to encounter an oasis in your life. Now is a time of awakening, renewal, and newfound delights. Expect a surge of creativity and opportunities to flow your way."

THE
MOON

There's a reason the term *lunacy* is derived from *lunar*. The Moon indicates confusion and being swayed by outside influences when you should be doing what you know is right in your heart. Thankfully, The Moon indicates you have a keen intuitive sense. It also indicates you have the wherewithal to do some honest soul-searching. Dive deep into your emotional waters to establish insight and emotional stability. Don't be confused by what the world is doing. Instead, follow your instincts and make your dreams come true. The time to make that happen is now.

When contemplating the meaning of The Moon, ask yourself:

How can I gain clarity of mind and purpose?

What is taking me away from my highest achievements?

Am I procrastinating? Why?

Do I value others' opinions more than my own? Why?

UPRIGHT

Intuition • Confusion • Persuasion • Right timing

REVERSE

Disbelief • Impatience • Frustration • Overemotional

Meaning in a Reading

UPRIGHT	REVERSE

Core Meaning

You're in the dark about some major decisions you need to make. No matter how much advice you ask for, the choice is ultimately yours. You're going to have to be confident in yourself. Trust your intuition. Stop wanting others to do the work for you.

Core Meaning

You're frustrated and impatient because you're not getting your way. Sober up and grow up. Start owning your behavior. If whatever you want is so important, then you're going to have to work for it.

Quick-Read Meanings

LOVE

There is a third person involved in your relationship and it's a big distraction. Find a harmonious way to deal with the intrusion, or move away from the love triangle.

MONEY

People are asking you for hand-outs, when they can easily do for themselves. Take the high road, and respectfully say no.

CAREER

Ignore what everybody else is doing. Stick to what you do best, and don't waver from your goals.

FAMILY

There's a lot going on in your home, and it has you pulled in way too many directions. Pick one or two priorities, and focus on these only.

Quick-Read Meanings

LOVE

You can't believe how you've been treated in a relationship. You feel wronged and hurt. Remind yourself you are worthwhile, and there are plenty more fish in the sea.

MONEY

You can't build a financial empire on dreams alone. It's time to put your money where your mouth is. Do the work, and get results.

CAREER

You've been drowning in a heavy workload, and it's affecting your performance. Work to catch up and delegate where you can.

FAMILY

Emotions run high, and there's not much you can do. Time is the only salve for the situation.

THE MOON

THE MOON SAYS...

"Believe in yourself and your dreams. Disappointment is only as debilitating as you make it. Dreams really do come true, but it takes conviction, self-honesty, and persistence. Be true to yourself, follow your instincts, and make your unique mark on this world."

THE
SUN

You're getting a new lease on life. Expect new beginnings and rejuvenation. Set your sights high because your future is bright and promising. Issues that held you back in the past are now cleared, and you have the energy to move forward with your goals. This is a highly positive card, and its presence in a reading suggests joy, healing, and good vibes.

When contemplating the meaning of The Sun, ask yourself:

- What's blocking me from joy and how can I remove the barrier?

- Am I paying attention to legitimate warning signs?

- Do I feel worthy of the good that flows to me?

- Is it time to grow up?

UPRIGHT

Freedom • Vitality • Celebration • Moving forward

REVERSE

Selfishness • Warning signs • Carelessness • Foolhardiness

Meaning in a Reading

UPRIGHT	REVERSE

Core Meaning

You are in a prime position to make and meet goals. Creativity is at full thrust. Communication is easy. Social gatherings, parties, and celebrations are in your future. Laughter, joy, and good health give you a fresh start.

Core Meaning

You are tempted to throw all cares to the wind and go full blast into a new direction. Your enthusiasm is blinding you to practical concerns. Avoid foolish mistakes by investing more thought in your actions. Take time to consider the needs of others.

Quick-Read Meanings

LOVE

New love is in the air and it looks promising. If you're already in a relationship, expect a sweet honeymoon phase.

MONEY

Investments are paying off. Take advantage of a great financial opportunity.

CAREER

Whatever was holding you back in the past is shifting to allow you forward mobility in your career. You've got the experience and qualifications to succeed.

FAMILY

Family celebrations are on the horizon. This is a sweet time of sharing, growth, and harmony. This card may also mean a happy new arrival in the family.

Quick-Read Meanings

LOVE

You bet on the wrong horse in a relationship, and now the mistake is glaringly obvious. Next time, don't be tempted to settle. You deserve more.

MONEY

Foolish spending is exposing you and others to some unsavory consequences. Wise up with your finances.

CAREER

You're getting mixed signals. You can avoid pitfalls if you get smart about hidden agendas at work.

FAMILY

Someone in the family is experiencing a stunt in development. You may need to find a tutor, or book an appointment with your family physician for a health check.

THE SUN

THE SUN SAYS...

"This is a time of renewal. You can reinvent yourself with ease. Things that held you back in the past are no longer an issue. Nurture the seeds of your dreams, and prepare to reap the harvest of your desires. Connect with your inner child and incorporate more play into your daily routines. Live, laugh, and love."

JUDGMENT

Often, the term *judgment* carries negative connotations, but the imagery of this card expresses positivity, freedom, and even a sense of rejoicing. Essentially, this card indicates a revolutionary verdict has been made in your favor. This ruling comes after a period of withdrawal, depression, or seclusion. An announcement is coming and it will have you jumping for joy. Or you'll receive news that you can move forward with an important project. In its simplest form, the Judgment card is a herald to "answer your highest calling."

When contemplating the meaning of Judgment, ask yourself:

What is my highest calling? Am I answering the call?

Am I judging myself or others too harshly?

If there was no chance of rejection, what action would I take?

How can I rise above confinement and be my best?

UPRIGHT

Relief • Good news • Discernment • Answered prayer

REVERSE

Rejection • Unfairness • Confinement • Self-conscious

Meaning in a Reading

UPRIGHT	REVERSE

Core Meaning

You have endured a time of deep contemplation, and have finally made a decision. You cleared out emotional baggage, and you can now make a clean break from past grudges. With introspection and self-investment you have attained balance, and your ability to discern better choices is keen.

Core Meaning

Somewhere along life's journey you decided you weren't worthy, and so you rejected the call to reach your higher potential. Extreme sensitivity to being in the spotlight, shyness, or embarrassment holds you back. Confining yourself in the shadows is not the answer.

Quick-Read Meanings

LOVE

You have been separated from a loved one for a long time. Expect to be reunited soon.

MONEY

News of an inheritance is coming your way. Old, forgotten investments surface and are now ripe for cashing.

CAREER

If you've been overlooked for a promotion, or are standing on the sidelines your time to shine is nigh.

FAMILY

Expect to be reunited with a loved one. He/she has been overseas or emotionally unreachable.

Quick-Read Meanings

LOVE

A severe case of bashfulness is keeping you from approaching a person to whom you are attracted. Take a chance.

MONEY

There's nothing wrong with being frugal, but you might be taking thrifty to the extreme.

CAREER

You're at a crossroads, and a case of self-doubt has you paralyzed. Rise above the fears and make the right choice in your career.

FAMILY

Sometimes a break is needed, but not at the expense of neglecting your family or isolating yourself from those who love you.

JUDGMENT

JUDGMENT SAYS...

"The old adage, 'it's always darkest before the dawn' is true in your case. You've had your fair share of struggle, and now you finally get a reprieve. Consider it a reward for hanging in there, keeping your faith, and doing your best to remain balanced through recent trials."

THE
WORLD

As the final card in the Major Arcana, The World stands for completion, satisfaction, and attainment. Over the course of your life experience, ups and downs have been plentiful, but you're now in a place of stability. You've achieved a great deal, and you're ready for whatever comes your way. You've gained self-confidence and success. You've met your goals and established structure in your life.

When contemplating the meaning of The World, ask yourself:

Will I be happy after I achieve all my goals?

How can I find ways to be happy with myself?

How can I be content with the way things are?

How can I maintain feelings of balance and satisfaction?

UPRIGHT

Completion • Satisfaction • Achievement • Resolution

REVERSE

Self-involved • Hindsight • Regret • Unwilling

Meaning in a Reading

UPRIGHT	REVERSE

Core Meaning

After enduring many experiences in life, you've obtained the skill, knowledge, and experience you need to be whole. You've come to the realization that you hold the power to create a dynamic, successful life.

Core Meaning

You've got to venture out, and take a few risks. Otherwise, you will look back on life and regret never having truly lived life. People want to help you because they care.

Quick-Read Meanings

LOVE

You know self-love is the ultimate love. In a relationship, you are a shining light. If not, you are totally comfortable being single.

MONEY

You may not be a millionaire, but you're certainly sitting pretty. You're in great financial shape.

CAREER

It took tremendous effort, but you're finally doing work you love. This is truly satisfying for you and those you serve.

FAMILY

Family is your pride, and the framework of your world. Enjoy this time in your life because your family is coming together and surrounds you with love.

Quick-Read Meanings

LOVE

If you think you're protecting yourself from a broken heart by building walls and hiding—you're wrong.

MONEY

You could be in better shape if you diversify. Relying on one source of income is adequate, but there are additional opportunities to explore.

CAREER

You've been doing the same thing for so long, you've become inflexible. Try branching out. Expand your skills.

FAMILY

Are you a family of one? This may feel lonely, but not having a biological family doesn't sentence you to isolation. Seek a support group; make your own family.

THE WORLD SAYS...

"You know your value, and it feels so good to be satisfied with how far you've come. You no longer have to prove yourself to others and you don't need others to confirm your worth either. You've attained the ultimate love ... self-love."

THE WORLD

THE SUIT OF
WANDS

ACE OF WANDS

This is the time to take affirmative action, and go where no man (or woman) has gone before. Explore new territories. Take initiative. Be fearless. Reach out to obtain your goals. Life is full of unknowns, but they don't have to hold you back from striving to achieve more.

When contemplating the meaning of The Ace of Wands, ask yourself:

Is giving up in my best interest?

How can I honor my passion?

How can I be more creative?

How can I be an inspiration to others?

Is it time to initiate new experiences and adventures?

UPRIGHT

Action • Assertion • Inspiration • Energizing

REVERSE

Ending • Stuck • Flat • Lackluster

Meaning in a Reading

UPRIGHT	REVERSE

Core Meaning

You are coming out of the fog and getting a glimpse of a better future for yourself. Inspiration is motivating you to move in a positive direction. You have clear vision about your goals, and have the energy to work toward them.

Core Meaning

You're stuck in a rut, and it's leaving you flat and unhappy. Some of this deflation is due to a few deals falling through at the last minute. You were banking on a good thing, but it went belly-up. Resist feelings of discouragement.

Quick-Read Meanings

LOVE

Someone is holding out an olive branch to you. Don't be stingy with your forgiveness. Consider accepting an apology.

MONEY

A potential investor is making you an offer. This is an opportunity to rekindle your financial fires.

CAREER

A bright idea puts you on top of your game. You might not be sure how to implement the idea, but you've got the makings of an ace venture.

FAMILY

Your family is facing a new beginning. Moving into a new home, a new addition to the family, or a new phase in family structure is on the horizon.

Quick-Read Meanings

LOVE

You're dealing with a very stubborn partner. He/she is unwilling to see your perspective. If you can't beat them, join them.

MONEY

You were certain you'd get a "thumbs up" for a financial proposal, but you got disapproval instead. Thankfully, there's more than one game in town. Try again.

CAREER

You want passion and value from your work. You can have that—but it might not come instantly. Stick it out and make the best of where you are now. Establishing a good track record will lead to better opportunities in the future.

FAMILY

Someone in your family has some very backward ideas about values. Approach him/her with love and patience. This member will eventually grow into a healthier understanding.

ACE OF WANDS

 THE ACE OF WANDS SAYS...

"A journey of a thousand experiences starts with one step forward. Take that first step into a brave, new world. Consider unconventional methods for reaching your goals. Be inspired. Get creative. Take hold of your life and awaken to new ideas."

TWO OF WANDS

You got your education and you're ready to take your newfound knowledge into the world. Whether you graduated from a conventional school, or from the school of life, you are definitely in a good position to teach others what you've learned.

When contemplating the meaning of The Two of Wands, ask yourself:

- What have I learned that I'm ready to share with the world?

- What are the pros and cons about the action I'm thinking of taking?

- Am I overconfident? Is there room for improvement?

- Is it time to initiate new experiences and adventures?

UPRIGHT

Choice • Teaching • Travel • Dreaming

REVERSE

Overconfident • Undetermined • Erratic

Meaning in a Reading

UPRIGHT	REVERSE

Core Meaning

You've got high ideals about what your future should look like. You've been dreaming about this day for a long time. You've prepared yourself to step out into the world. The only thing holding you back is making a choice about which direction to go.

Core Meaning

You're cocky about your future, but it would behoove you to take your ego down a notch. In reality, you've got a lot more room for improvement. When you develop more subtle forms of communicating who you are to the world, you'll see quick advancements.

Quick-Read Meanings

LOVE

Either you or a loved one need to move on. This might be a job offer in another town, or maybe one of you needs to move out of the relationship. It's not an easy choice, but it has to be made.

MONEY

You're faced with a tough decision. Stay in your current financial status, or make a huge leap. Making the leap is risky, but you can educate yourself to make the move less stressful.

CAREER

Don't be surprised if your company asks you to move abroad for your work. You've got obligations at home to consider. It's not going to be an easy offer to accept.

FAMILY

You've been thinking about returning home. This could be due to the need to oversee the family and reestablish order.

Quick-Read Meanings

LOVE

Your lack of empathy is causing a rift in your relationship. Stop and consider the needs of your partner. Pay attention, listen, and be more sensitive.

MONEY

There is an opportunity to make some money, but you're resistant to throw your hook in the pond. Cast your line already! That big fish is waiting, but you have to dive in first.

CAREER

That promotion or advancement could be within your reach, but you're going to have to earn it. No more resting on your laurels. Go back to school, or work to gain more experience.

FAMILY

Things seem topsy-turvy. Try establishing a daily or weekly routine within the family. This will help calm the chaos.

THE TWO OF WANDS SAYS...

"Pearls of wisdom are within you. It's time to crack your shell and share your luster with the world. Spread your ideas and make something of yourself. You have a vision; it's time to share it. You will be amazed at how much value you have to offer."

TWO OF WANDS

THREE OF WANDS

Although you are prepared to go to bat for the team, you are unable to do so. You have to delegate the action to others. Your value is in negotiating and giving instruction to your community. It's hard to stay behind while others fight the good fight on your behalf. However, your presence is needed more on the home front.

When contemplating the meaning of The Three of Wands, ask yourself:

How can I let go of things no longer serving me?

How can I be a better delegator and strategist?

How can I find peace with saying goodbye?

What is interfering with my vision?

UPRIGHT

Delegating • Strategy • Strength • Belief

REVERSE

Clinging • Flat-lining • Dejected • Self-pity

Meaning in a Reading

UPRIGHT	REVERSE

Core Meaning

You and a large faction of your peers share a common belief or goal. They have elected you leader, and you will have to send others out to do tasks you feel only you are equipped to handle. Now is the time to build strategies and let others employ them.

Core Meaning

You made some changes because you hoped for a better, more productive life. That's great, but you're clinging to old habits and it's thwarting new growth. You can't make progress if you stay in the past.

Quick-Read Meanings

LOVE

If you want to get noticed, you're going to have to take a stand. There is another person in the picture. Launch a plan to get his/her attention.

MONEY

Just because your finances aren't moving, doesn't mean you're immobilized. Detach from the situation to get a better vantage point.

CAREER

Dust off your résumé and letters of recommendation. It's time to send out your references and search for better opportunities.

FAMILY

Saying goodbye is never easy, but it's time to let go. Have faith you did right by your family, and give them your blessing as they leave the nest.

Quick-Read Meanings

LOVE

It's okay to lick your wounds for a time, but at some point you're going to have to pick yourself up and move on. Don't let rejection drown you in self-pity.

MONEY

You want the best money can buy. That's okay, as long as you aren't obsessed with materialism. Practice smart moderation, and make sure you have a healthy attitude about spending.

CAREER

You've been thinking about jumping ship and launching into a new field. Fear of leaving your comfort zone stops you. You'll never know what's out there if you don't explore your options.

FAMILY

Whether the old line "mom always loved you best" is true or not, it's time to get over sibling rivalry. You can't change your childhood. Forgive the errors in your upbringing and start living your life.

THREE OF WANDS

THE THREE OF WANDS SAYS...

"Maybe you are sending your children off to college. Perhaps loved ones are going off to the military. There is something precious in your life that is leaving for parts unknown. This doesn't mean goodbye forever. You can find ways to oversee, contribute, and add value."

FOUR OF WANDS

Weddings, family reunions, graduations—oh my! Be prepared for jolly good times ahead. It's time to celebrate life, love, and the presence of happiness. Passion and energy are reignited within the home and the bedroom. Signs indicate springtime, which is a time of conception and fertility.

When contemplating the meaning of The Four of Wands, ask yourself:

How can I prepare for home-comings and reunions?

What are my views about marriage?

How can I celebrate the beauty and love in my life?

How can I make my home a more welcoming environment?

UPRIGHT

Hope • Promise • Enthusiasm • Creativity

REVERSE

Extravagance • Ego-driven • Impropriety • Loss of perspective

Meaning in a Reading

UPRIGHT	REVERSE

Core Meaning

New beginnings, particularly in areas of home and family are blossoming. You have a newfound zest for life and enthusiasm. An influx of youthfulness imbues your life. The social butterfly within you is ready to fly, and the spirit of celebration prevails!

Core Meaning

You don't have to spend big to make people like you. The life you built on illusion, ego, and extravagance isn't a life of value. Gain perspective by spending on things that will last, like family, friendship, and charity in your community.

Quick-Read Meanings

LOVE

If there was ever a time to meet Mr. or Miss Right, it's right now! Your social gear is in high drive to encounter that special someone.

Quick-Read Meanings

LOVE

Somebody is being a show-off, and it's getting old. If you're the one bragging, back off and listen to your partner more. If your partner is the attention hound, remind him/her there is no "I" in "teamwork."

MONEY

Budding financial prospects come into bloom. Pay particular attention to real estate and property investments, as these are prime for plucking.

MONEY

Overspending is not advisable at this time. You may have a taste for opulence and luxury, but try to temper your appetite for a spell.

CAREER

Pick out the furniture and colors for your new office. You've made partner in the firm, got the accolades, and scored the deal that solidifies your position at work.

CAREER

You or somebody at work is behaving inappropriately. This makes the work environment awkward and uncomfortable. You can't ignore the behavior. Diplomatically try to restore decorum and professionalism.

FAMILY

Roll out the red carpet because family gatherings promise a royal good time. Start packing, too; that new house you've wanted is in your cards!

FAMILY

Loss of priorities in the family lead to severing ties and separations. It's not too late to counteract the damage. Unity can be achieved through mature, honest communication.

THE FOUR OF WANDS SAYS...

"Hope springs eternal! Spring is in the air, and with it comes an explosion of creativity and conception. Stop and smell the roses, engage in social activities, and savor time with family. If you're more comfortable as a wall flower, peel yourself off the bench and break out of shyness. Be careful not to overcompensate or over indulge in your festivities. This is an easy, breezy time in life. Enjoy every moment."

FIVE OF WANDS

You have strong beliefs and a powerful desire to defend your opinion. You're encountering resistance and not getting the support you expected. Disagreements, misunderstandings, and stand-offs are likely. Ironically, your peers share similar ideas. At the very least, there is common ground you share with the group. Take a different tack in presenting your ideas. Find commonalities and approach your tribe with intent to unify rather than divide.

When contemplating the meaning of The Five of Wands, ask yourself:

Do I always have to be right? Why?

Can I renegotiate the terms I agreed to?

Am I open and listening to other opinions?

How can I find common ground with others?

UPRIGHT

Willfulness • Resistance • Defense • Power struggle

REVERSE

Manipulation • Negotiating • Connecting • Pushing

Meaning in a Reading

UPRIGHT	REVERSE

Core Meaning

Although others recognize the value of your position, you're meeting resistance from the group. The project you are working on is replete with setbacks and road-blocks. Inspiration and creativity is staunched. Rather than fight through the barriers, try putting down your defenses and taking a more agreeable approach.

Core Meaning

"Inspiration, not perspiration" should be your motto. Work smarter, not harder. There is no shortage of ideas or brilliant projects to start—the problem is lack of support. Use your creative powers of persuasion to negotiate progress. There are smart ways to manipulate without being forceful or mean spirited.

Quick-Read Meanings

LOVE

You're trying to prepare for an event or party for your loved one, but nothing is coming together. There may be quarrels in the relationship about plans.

MONEY

The flow of finances is at a standstill, and you've run out of ideas to push through. Hunker down and conserve your resources.

CAREER

Your industry is volatile and unpredictable right now. You're running into closed doors, especially in areas of marketing and sales. Don't push it. This, too, shall pass.

FAMILY

Attempts to mend fences and build something of substance in the family aren't working. Let family members express their opinions and contribute to the household with their own unique style.

Quick-Read Meanings

LOVE

It feels like you're walking on your tippy toes around your partner. Don't push the issue, but definitely use finesse to find out what's bugging your mate.

MONEY

Your finances are like a round of piñata pouncing. You keep swinging your bat around wildly, but you're not hitting the prize. Take the blindfold off.

CAREER

There is a major fork in the road of your professional life. Use your business savvy to negotiate the best deal, and take the path that most suits your needs.

FAMILY

Don't be manipulated by persuasive family members. Don't allow yourself to be pushed around either. Call in recruits if you need strength or help dealing with a rebellious situation.

THE FIVE OF WANDS SAYS...

"Can you imagine a world of censorship, prohibition, and restriction? That's exactly what happens when you deny others the chance to express their own ideas and opinions. Communication, cooperation, negotiation—these are keywords when working with the group. Think outside the box, or else you're going to get boxed in a tight spot."

SIX OF WANDS

You've won the gold, but it wasn't easy. You had to persuade a lot of people, and jump through a lot of hoops to get the win. The biggest accomplishment through all this was treating your constituency with honesty and respect. Most people know a good leader when they witness one, and your true colors showed beautifully. You are going places, and you want to be sure your peers go with you. Enjoy your victory, and keep your altruistic ideals intact as you move forward.

When contemplating the meaning of The Six of Wands, ask yourself:

How can I maturely handle public acclaim and success?

Can I still listen to my own intuition, even when the advice from others is so strong?

Am I maintaining integrity and keeping my promises?

How can I avoid conflict and misdirection?

UPRIGHT

Valor • Integrity • Victory • Advancement

REVERSE

Misdirection • Rebellion • Irresponsibility • Antagonism

Meaning in a Reading

UPRIGHT	REVERSE

Core Meaning

You set your sights on the gold medal, and you achieved your objective. Your success was due in part by a large following of supporters. You gained these admirers by balancing your ego, maintaining integrity, and keeping promises. Plot your course to the next step, and maintain your stride to see your objective to full completion.

Core Meaning

You started a movement, but lost stamina. Now you're ditching responsibility. You're leaning toward three options: 1) Face your team and confess you can't finish the project; 2) Find a loophole or a shortcut to finish in half the time; 3) Run! Whichever tack you take, stick to it. There's no turning back from this one.

Quick-Read Meanings

LOVE

How flattering! You've gotten several propositions and requests for dates. But you know there is only one love for you. Go home with the one who took you to the dance in the first place.

MONEY

You played the ponies, and you won the gamble. Collect your winnings, and do the right thing by paying off a long-standing loan from an old friend.

CAREER

You won the hearts of the board of directors ... now what? Accept the new position with your head held high. You're obviously qualified for the new job. Be confident and live up to your potential.

FAMILY

A family member put a seemingly impossible demand upon you, but you came through. This put you in high esteem amongst the family and solidified your loyalty.

Quick-Read Meanings

LOVE

Snide remarks and sarcasm are a sign of passive-aggression. No matter how thick skinned you or your mate might be, there's no denying hurt feelings twitching under the surface.

MONEY

You lost your backing for a financial endeavor. It's a good thing you're resourceful and motivated. Start fund-raising independently.

CAREER

Morale is at an all-time low. Your co-workers are bailing out of the company. The temptation to follow the exodus is strong, but you're better served by sticking it out where you are.

FAMILY

Idle hands and too much free time can mean trouble for the young ones under your roof. Give the kids something to do.

SIX OF WANDS

THE SIX OF WANDS SAYS...

"Don't let success go to your head. You probably won't, because you'll remember all the hurdles and hard work it took to put you on top. Nevertheless, the voice of the people can sway you from taking the high road. Be honorable and listen to your inner guidance. Be true to yourself and your cause."

SEVEN OF WANDS

You won the match, but you're having to defend your title. Luckily, this isn't your first time in the ring. You're fully aware of your competition and have the confidence to deal with them. People who want what you have might jab at you. They are trying to knock you down a notch. You're capable of standing your ground. Nonetheless, defending yourself for too long can lead to exhaustion and procrastination. You may be unwilling to keep working so hard to maintain status quo.

When contemplating the meaning of The Seven of Wands, ask yourself:

Why am I procrastinating?

What is my leverage in this situation?

Am I exhibiting contradictory behavior?

Can I see a solution in which everybody wins?

Is there really a need to defend myself so vehemently?

UPRIGHT

Challenge • Defending • Willful • Justification

REVERSE

Weakness • Contradiction • Inferiority • Lack of substance

Meaning in a Reading

UPRIGHT	REVERSE

Core Meaning

You feel like you have to justify your position. It's okay to defend your beliefs. You earned your status. However, be mindful of the methods you use to stay on top. Violence and anger are immature, ineffective ways to meet challenges. Instead, try holding your ground with integrity, level-mindedness, and strong will.

Core Meaning

Stress is high and footing is shaky. Too many people are pulling you in too many directions. You tend to agree with people when you really don't. You say yes to favors when you should say no and focus on your own needs first. All this has you wanting to escape. Resist the urge to run away or rely on substances to deal with pressure.

Quick-Read Meanings

LOVE

A shift in your attitude has suitors lined up at your door. Be selective about who you date or keep relations with. Say no to anyone who isn't prepared to offer you what you deserve.

MONEY

You're on pins and needles about your financial standing. Instead of worrying about lack, stand up and take action against the fear.

CAREER

You said one thing, but did another. Your co-workers and associates noticed. You're being called on mistakes. Stand up and straighten out the confusion.

FAMILY

Everybody has their own ideas about how the household should run. This causes squabbles and confusion. Work to unify the ranks and find common ground.

Quick-Read Meanings

LOVE

Your mate put you on a pedestal. Nobody is perfect, and it's not fair to have a lover put unobtainable expectations on you. Stop fighting to meet his/her ideal of you, and start being yourself.

MONEY

You owe money to people and they're getting impatient for payment. Pay up now. If you can't, try to negotiate better terms.

CAREER

You took credit for someone else's work, or you didn't give credit where credit was due. Tell the truth about it, because the white lie will be discovered.

FAMILY

A family member is feeling insecure about his/her standing with you. Address this now. Give assurance you are there for this person. Otherwise his/her inferiority complex could get unhealthy.

THE SEVEN OF WANDS SAYS...

"It's time to pick your battles. Fame, status, and materialism might not be worth fighting for. Love, respect, and relationships are. Look within and determine what is most important to you. Then make a stand and fight to defend your right to live the life you deserve."

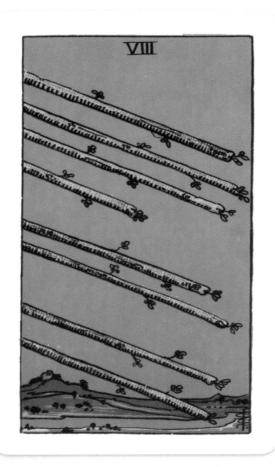

EIGHT OF WANDS

The signs are clear. At least they should be, if you're paying attention. The Eight of Wands indicates a message, a sign, a signal of what direction to take. Clues are being dropped for you about how to move forward. These indicators may point to emotional security or home life. Other meanings include travel, relocation, and receipt of important news.

When contemplating the meaning of The Eight of Wands, ask yourself:

Is it time for a break?

Am I sure about my direction?

Am I ready to receive the message?

Is it time for a trip or relocation?

Am I being direct in my message to others?

UPRIGHT

Aim • Message • Direction • Balance

REVERSE

Discord • Frustration • Giving up • Unknown

Meaning in a Reading

UPRIGHT	REVERSE

Core Meaning

News is coming that will lend new insight and perspective. This information is the missing piece you've been waiting for. It could facilitate travel or a move you've been wanting to make. Use the information to better yourself and maintain balance in your life.

Core Meaning

You've been doing a lot of emotional push-ups lately. Maybe it's time to take a break or change your routine. Doing this will allow anxiety to ease up and gets your life flowing easier. You're just stepping back until balance is reestablished.

Quick-Read Meanings

LOVE

Your partner is pointing an accusing finger at you. Either you're not at fault, or you're dodging the accusation. Get proof that substantiates your side of the story.

MONEY

Get on the straight and narrow path with your finances. Balance needs to be established.

CAREER

Keep your nose to the grindstone. Stick to the direction you've been working for until further notice. You'll soon be getting word that will help your next career move.

FAMILY

For a change, everybody is on the same page. There is full agreement within the household about the next move the family should take.

Quick-Read Meanings

LOVE

Characteristics about your mate you once found endearing or inspirational now seem like character flaws. Be fair. Decide whether you can live with these traits or not, and make your move.

MONEY

You're waiting on money, but its arrival isn't guaranteed. Time to stop waiting for your fortune to magically change, and start changing it with your own actions.

CAREER

You're climbing the ladder to success. You have a lot of unanswered questions about your ascent. Some of these are moral issues you're struggling with. All you can do is do your best.

FAMILY

While others might be looking down their noses at how you run your family affairs, rest assured—you're doing just fine. Don't let gossip frustrate you.

EIGHT OF WANDS

THE EIGHT OF WANDS SAYS...

"Life is full of parallels. For example, something a friend is experiencing 1,000 miles away might be similar to what you're going through. The universe sends you messages from all kinds of sources. These signs and similarities point to various directions you can take in life. Be observant and focused. Pay attention to cues that help you make decisions for your advancement."

NINE OF WANDS

My how the scenery has changed! You may have started from humble beginnings, but you're far away from those roots now. Even so, you've kept your values and vision. Standing up for your dreams and beliefs has been trying. You've had to duke it out, defend yourself, and lick your wounds. Battle-worn as you might be, take heart. You have the support you need to see your vision through.

When contemplating the meaning of The Nine of Wands, ask yourself:

Who has my back? Am I supported?

How can I reinforce my position?

What can I learn from previous challenges?

How can I prepare myself for the next wave of challenges?

UPRIGHT

Resolute • Determined • Building • Support

REVERSE

Mental decline • Unsteady • Unstructured • Failure

Meaning in a Reading

UPRIGHT	REVERSE

Core Meaning

You've had to apply some major elbow grease to build structure. This could mean construction work, or it could be building a foundation for a worthy cause. You may be weary from the work, but you're doing a great job. Keep up the good work.

Core Meaning

Einstein said the definition of insanity is doing the same thing over and over, but expecting different results. That pretty much sums up the meaning of this reversed card. Your efforts are admirable, but bucking the system is futile.

Quick-Read Meanings

LOVE

Disagreements in a long-standing relationship have you troubled. Should you stay or go? You've got an amazing support group; get advice from them.

MONEY

You have plenty of financial backing, but you feel it's best to strike out on your own. It won't be easy, but you'll be satisfied with independence.

CAREER

Being a rebel with a cause can be worthwhile, but risky. Using your career as a platform for reform will be a lonely path. Stay resolute even if you lose friends and associates.

FAMILY

The black sheep of the family is more of an outcast than usual. He/she isn't helping matters by being willful and obstinate. You can try to offer support, but it likely won't be accepted.

Quick-Read Meanings

LOVE

You're having to nurse your loved one back to health. As you tend to physical ailments, be mindful of his/her emotional and mental recovery, too.

MONEY

A few financial seeds you planted failed, but that doesn't spoil the whole crop. Keep planting; your money crop isn't as fallow as you think.

CAREER

Unsteady footing at work has you feeling wounded and dejected. Work to employ structure and routine. This will help your attitude as well as performance.

FAMILY

There's an elephant in the room, and nobody is willing to talk about it. It's no use sweeping the issue under the rug, because it's going to keep resurfacing.

NINE OF WANDS

THE NINE OF WANDS SAYS...

"Anything worthwhile is worth fighting for. You may need to call in reinforcements to accomplish your goals. The path you take will catapult you in a completely different direction than you expected. Be proud of the progress you've made so far. Count your war wounds as badges of courage."

TEN OF WANDS

You've been busy! You've spent a long time—perhaps a lifetime—gathering ideas, resources, and tools. Now you're ready to put all your life experiences and resources to work. You'll do this in practical ways. Areas of homesteading, environment, and community will benefit from your knowledge. Be careful not to shoulder all the responsibility in your endeavors. Let others help you with your goals.

When contemplating the meaning of The Ten of Wands, ask yourself:

What have I learned that can be applied in a practical way?

Am I overtaxed? Overextending? Overburdened?

What's blocking my vision?

Am I being selfish?

How can I contribute to and honor my roots?

UPRIGHT

Collecting • Centered • Determination • Homecoming

REVERSE

Hoarding • Selfish • Immature • Blind

Meaning in a Reading

UPRIGHT	REVERSE

Core Meaning

Whether coins, stamps, or inspiration—you've accumulated an impressive collection. You feel compelled to put your acquisitions to work. This might mean selling off your valuable collection to pay off a mortgage.

Core Meaning

Reversed, this card sends a petulant, schoolyard message that goes something like: "No fair! I'm taking all my toys and going home!" Somebody stepped on your feelings, and your reaction is to withdraw or take.

Quick-Read Meanings

LOVE

You're holding all the cards in the relationship and your partner is out of the game. It's your call if you want to give him/her a second chance in the relationship.

MONEY

You're being stingy with your money and resources. Or worse, you've gotten downright greedy. Consider giving to families in need or to environmental causes..

CAREER

After obtaining an education abroad, you are ready to return to your roots and share your knowledge. Your newly attained experience will be an innovating influence.

FAMILY

You or someone in the family is shouldering all the responsibility. Make sure all members are pitching in and chores are distributed equally.

Quick-Read Meanings

LOVE

You'd rather stay blind to the truth. You are selfishly denying your partner the opportunity to speak candidly.

MONEY

Watch your tendency to hoard your holdings. It's no sin to save, but there's a fine line between frugality and greed.

CAREER

You've got your finger on the pulse of your industry. You're in a powerful position of control. Be mindful not to be overburdened by work. Try to share and delegate the load.

FAMILY

Declare a national "hug your family members" day. There's a need for physical reassurance and affection. If touch doesn't come naturally to you, give it a try for the sake of your family.

THE TEN OF WANDS SAYS...

"If you pile the kindling too high in your arms, you can't see the path that leads to fire. If you hold onto things that don't serve you, you're going to miss all the fun in life. Life is about giving and receiving. Make sure you have a centered grasp on that concept."

PAGE OF WANDS

The world is your oyster, and you know it. You have a touch of destiny about you. Your creative engines are revved up with high octane self-expression. This is a time in your life where your vision becomes a reality. You're seeking ways to show off your talents. This is achieved through social connection, service to others, and higher education. Travel is particularly effective for personal development and getting in touch with your free spirit.

When contemplating the meaning of The Page of Wands, ask yourself:

If I unleash my full creative force, where will it lead?

How can I introduce more style and art in my life?

Is it time to launch that creative idea I've been dreaming about?

UPRIGHT

Dreaming • Traveling • Artistic • Admiration

REVERSE

Lazy • Exploiting • Snobby • Fickle

Meaning in a Reading

UPRIGHT	REVERSE

Core Meaning

This page implies you're getting assistance with a creative project. Your sense of style is enhanced. Expect heightened imagination that will take you to new levels of focus. Newfound appreciation for the arts is likely. Dreaming leads to innovative ideas. This Page also bestows promise of exciting adventures in travel.

Core Meaning

You or someone you know may be incredibly talented, but bragging about it is alienating. There is a tendency to rely exclusively on past success, which leads to a stagnated future. Being a creative genius doesn't give permission to be a snob, exploit others, or be lazy.

Quick-Read Meanings

LOVE

Add some sophistication to your relationship. Spice up your date night with a trip to an art museum or attend a Shakespearian play.

MONEY

That enterprise you've been wanting to launch is likely to succeed. You'll receive funding for your endeavor in unexpected places.

CAREER

Consider launching your own business. Entrepreneurial ventures in fashion, graphic design, and culinary arts are highly viable for you at this time.

FAMILY

Expect visitors from out of town to grace your home. Your guests will invigorate your household and provide new ideas to inspire your family.

Quick-Read Meanings

LOVE

Someone in the relationship is taking advantage of the other. Don't let a fickle lover put a dent in your self-confidence.

MONEY

A flippant attitude toward your finances has you unmotivated to work. Resting on your laurels is okay for a time, but financial growth rarely happens without effort.

CAREER

You might be excellent at your job, but making others feel inferior causes tension. Don't lose focus on the value others provide. Do your best to employ healthy teamwork tactics.

FAMILY

Inconsistencies in the family cause frustration. Rules once in place are not being upheld or reinforced. This sends mixed messages to the family.

PAGE OF WANDS

THE PAGE OF WANDS SAYS...

"Style, panache, and artistic flair are vital elements to success. Paying attention to fine details and adding creative touches will convert ordinary experiences into extraordinary ones. Consider taking a trip to jump-start your imagination. Your creativity is at an all-time high; take advantage of it. Dreaming big pays off, but don't lose sight of foundational values. Expect good news regarding innovation and progress."

KNIGHT OF WANDS.

KNIGHT OF WANDS

Get out the fire extinguishers because you are smoking! The lightning bolt of inspiration has struck and you feel electrified by new opportunities. You've got a radiant idea you're ready launch into action. Travel is a key factor in manifesting your dreams. You are on a quest. Your mission will allow you to explore creative realms within your heart and in your environment. This card implies there is nothing holding you back from your desires.

When contemplating the meaning of The Knight of Wands, ask yourself:

How can I make my passions work *for* me, not against me?

How can I get more inspired and motivated?

Am I mature enough to take charge?

Am I letting anger get the best of me?

UPRIGHT

Passion • Belief • Manifestation • Determination

REVERSE

Anger • Ego • Overzealous • Delay

Meaning in a Reading

UPRIGHT	REVERSE

Core Meaning

The Knight of Wands is fueled by passion. In a reading, this card implies getting excited and taking charge of your future. It deals with turning your dreams into a reality with enthusiastic action. Renewed inspiration and passion are the prime elements for your success.

Core Meaning

Your passion is admirable, but you didn't consider all the details before you charged forward. You allowed your ego to do the walking instead of taking a rational, balanced approach. This has caused delays and frustration in your progress. Keep your enthusiasm, but temper it with common sense.

Quick-Read Meanings

LOVE

If you want your ideal relationship, you've got to go for the gusto. Take the plunge, and dive into your love life with confidence and passion.

MONEY

Money is manifesting in your life after a long drought. Your financial status seemed bleak before, but now you are experiencing renewed wealth.

CAREER

Hard work and determination are foundational for your upward mobility in your career. Incorporate more creativity in your actions, and you'll see quick progress.

FAMILY

There's a rebel in the family who has some radical ideas. Be as supportive as you can while reminding this person about the practical side of reality.

Quick-Read Meanings

LOVE

Someone put the brakes on your love life, and things are at a screeching halt. Step back and reevaluate. Your highly charged charisma may have scared off the object of your affection.

MONEY

Your finances seem to be in the dust, and there doesn't appear to be an oasis in sight. A break is coming your way, but you'll have to roam the desert a little longer.

CAREER

You let anger get the best of you. Granted, unfair action was taken against you; but getting mad and acting out isn't going to advance your career.

FAMILY

Someone you looked up to in the family has let you down. Realize everybody is human—even role models—and try to forgive.

THE KNIGHT OF WANDS SAYS...

"You're so ready for fast-forward action that everything in your life feels at a stand-still. Resist the urge to forge blindly ahead. It's wonderful you are so on fire with passion and excitement. However, pay attention to common sense and practicalities. Creativity is most powerful when it's employed with forethought and maturity."

KNIGHT OF WANDS

QUEEN OF WANDS

You take great pride in your social standing. How friends and family perceive you is important. Luckily, most of your social networks see you as bright, intelligent, and perceptive. Your connection with others through service and support makes you thrive. Strength, honor, and integrity are the tenets by which you live your life. You have a positive outlook on life. This is due to your creative spirit and a keen reliance upon intuition. You're like a magnet for great things. Your strong expectation attracts wonderful things to you.

When contemplating the meaning of The Queen of Wands, ask yourself:

How can I maintain positive influence in my community?

How can I be more observant and look out for more creative outlets?

How can I encourage more love and healing?

What's the hidden solution here?

UPRIGHT

Positivity • Growth • Expectation • Intuition

REVERSE

Gossip • Hardened • Cold • Domineering

Meaning in a Reading

UPRIGHT	REVERSE

Core Meaning

The Queen of Wands sits on the throne of intuition and encourages you to put your sixth sense in a position of authority. Trust your instinct, and follow your impulses. You are in a positive place for growth, healing, and inspiration. Your creative endeavors are protected, and you are divinely guided on your path.

Core Meaning

Although it may be true that things haven't gone your way, don't harden your heart. Recent losses or disappointments have you feeling cold and disconnected. A crises in faith compels you to withdraw and isolate. To compensate, you may want to dominate others to feel control over your situation.

Quick-Read Meanings

LOVE

Your pride is your relationships. You know how to take care of your partner, and your efforts are appreciated. You're making a big impact in matters of love.

MONEY

You're expecting a ruling or decision to go your way which will mean a financial gain in your future.

CAREER

You are in a position of authority which requires you to hold your head high and keep your integrity intact. Someone may try to stall your creativity, but trust your instinct.

FAMILY

Your family is experiencing a beautiful time of trust and growth. Family is a great source of pride for you. The more you invest, the more your family will thrive.

Quick-Read Meanings

LOVE

You had high hopes for a relationship, but its deterioration has crushed your spirit. Take heart; love will kneel at your throne again soon.

MONEY

You didn't trust your instincts, and therefore missed out on winning a tidy chunk of change. No use dwelling on the loss. Listen to your intuition next time.

CAREER

Gossip at the office makes you feel like an outsider. It's all senseless prattle with no merit. Just be yourself, maintain your integrity, and pay no mind to the busybodies.

FAMILY

The black sheep of the family has reformed his/her ways, and now wants back into the fold. Try not to let past hurt feelings harden your heart to him/her. Forgive and forget.

THE QUEEN OF WANDS SAYS...

"You are in a positive position to support your loved ones and bring about hope in your community. Be firm, yet loving as you guide others. Use your intuition in social settings. Many people look to your leadership; you have the ability to change lives for the better. Be aware of your strong influence, and keep a loving heart."

KING OF WANDS.

KING OF WANDS

This is the king of fire and inspiration. In a reading, this card indicates you are passionate about being a leader. You don't let little things like distractions or setbacks cloud your vision. People look up to you because of your enthusiasm and powerful influence. Your charisma is infectious and you're a natural at coaching others. Your kindness, protection, and support for other people makes you well loved and respected. This is a big source of self-worth. You take great pride in being an appreciated member of your community.

When contemplating the meaning of The King of Wands, ask yourself:

Am I following my instincts?

Do I leap to conclusions and overreact too much? Why?

How can I protect my assets in healthy ways?

Am I a good provider and guardian?

How can I gain control to make a positive impact?

UPRIGHT

Influence • Instinct • Preparedness • Protection

REVERSE

Immature • Intolerant • Irresponsible • Impatient

Meaning in a Reading

UPRIGHT	REVERSE

Core Meaning

You have built a grand kingdom. You've taken risks and invested time and hard work to be king. Your job now is to reinforce your authority with integrity and honesty. Overseeing and protecting your investments is a priority. Use your instinct for guidance. Be aware of outside influences, and take fair action when you see fit.

Core Meaning

You're unhappy with how events have unfolded, and you're behaving badly in response. Your frustration is understandable, but lashing out and exploding like a loose cannon won't solve anything. Try to regain your poise and composure. Being calm is key for regaining control.

Quick-Read Meanings

LOVE

Your partner may seem domineering and overprotective. This could be uncomfortable, but your partner doesn't realize he/she is being overbearing. Have an honest discussion about it.

MONEY

You recently experienced a boost in status and wealth. This is great, but it's going to take hard work to stay balanced. Keep a tight grip on your morals and values.

CAREER

Co-workers, partners, and associates are keeping a close eye on you. What they see is a polished leader, and someone who deserves respect. Have no doubt about your value as an authority in your career.

FAMILY

Pay homage to the patriarch of the family. It's time to give the father figure in your life recognition and a gesture of gratitude.

Quick-Read Meanings

LOVE

The mate you fell in love with has turned into a chameleon. Have a talk to uncover why his/her behavior has become shifty and unusual.

MONEY

Exerting too much control over your money has lead to obsessive thoughts. Try to relax a little. Make your money work for you, but don't be a slave to it.

CAREER

The big boss has been overthrown, and you may be up for his/her job. Think hard about your readiness to fill the shoes of your predecessor.

FAMILY

Intolerance and impatience in the home has everyone on edge. Your frustration is understandable, but could be avoided if more structure is put in place.

THE KING OF WANDS SAYS...

"It's good to be king, especially when things go smoothly. The real challenge is protecting value when the road gets rocky. Avoid knee-jerk reactions or overcompensating when situations aren't going the way you expect. The honor of being in authority is earned when you rule with fairness and altruism."

KING OF WANDS

THE SUIT OF PENTACLES

ACE OF PENTACLES.

ACE OF PENTACLES

In a world replete with distractions and questionable motives, it's easy to get knocked out of balance. This card encourages stability, and is a promise that a better way of life is possible. Take initiative to introduce simple, wholesome values in your daily life. Be grateful for things you might usually take for granted like a roof over your head, running water, sunshine, and food on the table. Recognizing these small blessings puts you on a positive path and opens the gateway to more abundance.

When contemplating the meaning of The Ace of Pentacles, ask yourself:

Do I feel deserving of the gifts I receive?

How can I embrace opportunities?

Have I laid the groundwork for my best interest?

Am I counting my blessings?

Are distractions keeping me off-balance?

UPRIGHT

Cooperation • Stability • Prosperity • Promise

REVERSE

Refusal • Unlucky • Stalled • Jealousy

Meaning in a Reading

UPRIGHT	REVERSE

Core Meaning

Be prepared to have your material needs met. New experiences are opening up to support your needs. Chance meetings with important people and lucky breaks are in your future. Take advantage of opportunities. Cooperate with events conspiring to assist you in bettering your life.

Core Meaning

You've been granted opportunities, but you turned them down. Maybe you're untrusting. Perhaps you fear advancement. Your refusal to accept good things has you stalled, bitter, and feeling lousy. You could prosper, too, but you have to stop justifying your position of lack.

Quick-Read Meanings

LOVE

Your love relationship is moving to the next level. Some potential advancements include marriage, sharing a home together, or perhaps raising a child.

MONEY

You are in line to receive a gift that could really help your material standing. Don't think of yourself as a charity case. Accept the gift with gratitude and grace.

CAREER

You've been working toward a specific career goal. Good news—you're extremely close to reaching that goal. Promotions, advancements, and better options are on the horizon.

FAMILY

Initiate beautification! Start a garden, buy a better home, or refinance or remodel your existing home. Bettering your environment will make a positive impact on your family.

Quick-Read Meanings

LOVE

Your luck in relationships hasn't been the greatest lately. That will change as soon as you admit you've been settling. You deserve better.

MONEY

You took a few risks, and now you're paying for it. You have a chance to salvage the damage by uncovering the details you missed before.

CAREER

An associate got the promotion you were gunning for. Naturally, this might evoke feelings of jealousy. Try to be happy for your co-worker, and recognize your day in the sun will come, too.

FAMILY

For whatever reasons, you've been stingy with your time and attention. Stop justifying time away from your family, and start giving yourself to them more.

 THE ACE OF PENTACLES SAYS...

"The Ace of Pentacles indicates an initiation into new directions that offer splendid opportunity. Don't overlook small blessings, because they could lead to very big things. A shift in fortune doesn't have to hit you over the head like a ton of bricks to be valuable or revolutionary. A flood starts with a small trickle. The same holds true with your prosperity."

TWO OF PENTACLES

If you're looking for steady and predictable you're not going to find it—at least not right now. This is a time of ups and downs in finances and material status. The highs and lows of life don't have to rock your world in a bad way. You can use the swing tide to your advantage. Be mindful of opportunities lurking in unlikely places. This time can also be a great education in maintaining balance in unstable conditions.

When contemplating the meaning of The Two of Pentacles, ask yourself:

What can I do to juggle responsibilities better?

Am I prepared to be held accountable for my actions?

How can I apply my higher ideals?

How can I better handle the good with the bad?

UPRIGHT

Juggling • Balance • Renewal • Karma

REVERSE

Drama • Unaccountable • Undependable • Irresponsible

Meaning in a Reading

UPRIGHT	REVERSE

Core Meaning

You may notice consequences of past actions surfacing. You might also feel like you're having to juggle many different tasks in order to maintain balance in your life. Luckily, for every low there is a high. If you're in the low tide of life, hang in there—you're bound to experience an upswing soon.

Core Meaning

Choices in the past were made selfishly, without considering consequences. These choices have caught up with you, and have put you in a tailspin. Being accountable and responsible for your actions is the ideal solution. Eliminating dramatic reactions to your plight is also advisable.

Quick-Read Meanings

LOVE

You're torn between two lovers, and perhaps feeling like a fool. Avoid karmic payback, and do the right thing. Be fair and honest to both parties.

MONEY

Now more than ever, it's vital to balance your bank account. You overlooked a small detail in your finances that could lead to big gains if you reconcile it.

CAREER

You're at a crossroads and questioning your career choices. Consider a trade in environmental conservation or travel. You're going to get advice from a long-distance source that will give you clarity.

FAMILY

You've had to wear a lot of hats to keep the home in order. Now it's time for another member of the family to take a little control. Let him/her establish balance.

Quick-Read Meanings

LOVE

You gambled in love and lost. Your only recourse is to accept the blow, and take better care of future relationships.

MONEY

Due to irresponsible managing of funds, you are suffering a financial blow. Thankfully, what goes down must come up. Aim for dependability in your accounting and you'll see a positive financial reversal.

CAREER

You may be displaying inappropriate and erratic behavior at work. Perhaps emotional issues are affecting your performance. Do your best to keep the drama at home. Work is no place to air dirty laundry.

FAMILY

Shirking responsibility is causing dire consequences in the family. There's nothing wrong with having fun, but not at the cost of your family's stability.

TWO OF PENTACLES

THE TWO OF PENTACLES SAYS...

"In a world that seems out of control, it's nice to know you can control some things. You can apply high-minded awareness to manipulate events in your life. This is done by making conscious choices that put you on a noble path of success. Celebrate the things you can change, and employ wisdom to recognize the things you can't."

THREE OF PENTACLES

Be prepared to show off your stuff, and get noticed. You're going to have a chance to express yourself, pitch your ideas, and present your craftsmanship to very important parties. The work you do now to impress people in power will pay off in your future. This is a time of great opportunity and advancement.

When contemplating the meaning of The Three of Pentacles, ask yourself:

Do I believe in myself and my talents?

Am I prepared to work hard to get what I want?

How can I make a great impression and get noticed?

Am I getting good advice?

What steps can I take to advance my success?

UPRIGHT

Success • Hard work • Getting noticed • Growth

REVERSE

Overworked • Mistrusting • Plateau • Interference

Meaning in a Reading

UPRIGHT	REVERSE

Core Meaning

You have confidence in your work, and you should be very enthusiastic about your prospects. Creativity leads to great opportunity. Winning bids, landing contracts, and securing new business is highly likely. Having faith in your abilities gives you a winning attitude and a leg-up in your work.

Core Meaning

Building an empire isn't easy—especially when all your hard work seems to go unnoticed. You're experiencing a plateau, which is frustrating because no matter how much you invest, business seems flat. Colleagues and friends are well-meaning with their advice, but don't trust everything they say. Outside opinions may interfere and suppress your progress.

Quick-Read Meanings

LOVE

You might be feeling like a third wheel. A third party in your relationship like a child or parent could be a help or a hindrance depending on your reactions.

MONEY

Long overdue payments are rolling in for work done in the past. Now is the time to collect on old debts.

CAREER

This is your Midas touch moment. The work you do now promises big business and industry. Keep a winning attitude, because your career is enjoying a time of profit and prosperity.

FAMILY

Get some professional advice or family counseling. You've worked hard to build a solid foundation, but now a third party is required to weigh in on the situation.

Quick-Read Meanings

LOVE

Troubles with in-laws are coming to a boil. You can try avoiding conflict, but addressing meddlesome behavior with candor and kindness is the best tack.

MONEY

Bad financial advice has you working double-time to recoup. You'll get back in the black, but it will take time.

CAREER

You lack faith in your own ability and skills. Rather than bemoan this sudden lack of confidence, pick yourself up and prove to yourself that you have what it takes to succeed.

FAMILY

A family member confessed to a betrayal, and it hit you like a hammer. It's okay if you need to take time to process the news.

THE THREE OF PENTACLES SAYS...

"All work and no play isn't boring at all when you are having a ball! Success and progress inspire you to work harder and get noticed by investors and admirers alike. Devotion to honing your craft and skills takes on a spiritual importance to you as you see the value in a job well done. There is no greater reward than making a positive difference in the work by your own efforts."

FOUR OF PENTACLES

You find yourself in a position of great power. It's important to know that with great power comes great responsibility. You're called upon to distribute resources to a group or community. You must do this with fairness and conscientiousness. Don't let power corrupt you or allow greed to set in.

When contemplating the meaning of The Four of Pentacles, ask yourself:

Am I being fair and responsible with money?

How can I give more to my community?

What have I done to deserve isolation?

Am I taking my role as a leader seriously?

Do I fully understand my influence in the community?

UPRIGHT

Control • Influence • Philanthropy • Status

REVERSE

Closed • Outcast • Loss • Disapproval

Meaning in a Reading

UPRIGHT	REVERSE

Core Meaning

Whether it's coaching your baseball team or managing a metropolis, every move you make for the sake of the group is vitally important. People are depending on you to execute sound judgment. You have impressive resources at your disposal. Don't take your duties lightly. There is more at stake than you know.

Core Meaning

You or someone you know has serious issues with materialism. Money has become a false idol; its importance overshadows all else. This will eventually lead to emotional collapse, loss of resources, and alienation.

Quick-Read Meanings

LOVE

Don't make the trappings of a partnership more important than a healthy relationship. For example, don't be tempted to marry for money—marry for love.

MONEY

You have your finger on the pulse of major money and resources. Be responsible with how you utilize your monetary power. Consider philanthropy and charity.

CAREER

The needs of many outweigh your own needs. Self-sacrifice is the theme in your work. There is no room for selfish action.

FAMILY

Take a hard look at how you influence your family. Are you setting a good example? Your family is watching you, and depending on you for moral stability.

Quick-Read Meanings

LOVE

Disagreements about money and resources cause a rift in your relationship. If you are undergoing a divorce, expect hitches and difficulties in getting a fair settlement.

MONEY

Placing too much importance on money backfires. Clinging too tightly to money will lead to loss of it.

CAREER

Maybe it wasn't totally your fault, but you made a move at work that met with disapproval from your superiors. You can regain respect by standing firm on company policy.

FAMILY

If you find yourself an outcast from the family, take a long look at your own actions. The responsibility lies squarely on your shoulders. Try to make amends.

THE FOUR OF PENTACLES SAYS...

"The laws of life are based on give and take. There are going to be times in your life when it feels like you have to give more than usual. Rest assured that you will eventually receive rewards for your generosity. You have a golden opportunity to implement wonderful and positive changes that will influence generations to come."

FIVE OF PENTACLES

Sometimes you have to hit rock bottom before you can bounce back. Pulling this card indicates you have experienced a series of misfortunes that have set you back. You are left out in the cold, and feel shunned by society. It feels like others have turned their back on you and you have nowhere to turn. This is a harsh winter of your life. The good news is seasons change, and spring will return. The bad news is you're going to have to endeavor and struggle through the discomfort for a time.

When contemplating the meaning of The Five of Pentacles, ask yourself:

What lessons could I have learned from the past?

What is the condition of my faith?

What are my priorities?

What is truly important to me?

How can I get back on track?

UPRIGHT

Dejected • Poverty • Illness • Faith

REVERSE

Spirituality • Transition • Priorities • Belief

Meaning in a Reading

UPRIGHT	REVERSE

Core Meaning

Losing everything can mean a significant gain in perspective. If you are dealing with loss, illness, and/or hardship, you may find you only have faith to cling to. Heavy reliance on spiritual ideals will get you through harrowing difficulties.

Core Meaning

You are going through a major transition that will galvanize your beliefs and strengthen your spirituality. Where priorities were vague or misaligned in the past, this is now not the case. You are quite clear about what is important, and you are ready to make changes for the better.

Quick-Read Meanings

LOVE

Times are lean and tough, but at least you can lean on your partner for support. In this case, love will save you.

MONEY

You're starting to recognize the value of money now that you don't have it. Current financial duress is a lesson in being more responsible with resources in the future.

CAREER

Failure with job searches and lack of opportunity is disheartening. Don't use failure as justification for quitting. Keep plodding forward.

FAMILY

Your family may be down and out right now, but there is light at the end of the tunnel. Don't be too proud to accept help.

Quick-Read Meanings

LOVE

You are finally starting to heal after a bitter betrayal. You are beginning to believe you can love again.

MONEY

Money status is in transition and unstable. Try not to worry if your prospects appear bleak. Your outlook should improve soon.

CAREER

Try knocking on a door that was closed to you in the past. Where you were once redundant, a change in industry has now made you valuable.

FAMILY

Strong values and belief in family ties have gotten your clan through a lot of transition and hardship. You are living proof that a family who prays together, stays together.

THE FIVE OF PENTACLES SAYS...

"You may be down and out, but you're far from defeated. You're learning some hard lessons. Use this phase in life to look back on the good times and make a promise to never take things for granted again. When your fortune changes for the better (and it will), give thanks and give credit where it is due. This is a period in your life when you have an opportunity to experience tremendous spiritual awakening. Use misfortune to strengthen your faith and beliefs."

SIX OF PENTACLES

Often you have to give in order to receive. You have been through enough trials and tribulations to know this. After enduring major hardships and setbacks in your life, you now have the ability to be sensitive to the needs of others. You have also worked hard to be in a position to help others in their time of need.

When contemplating the meaning of The Six of Pentacles, ask yourself:

- Am I being responsible with my resources?
- How can I offer balanced solutions to the community?
- How can I influence positive change?
- How do I feel about charity?
- Do I have a sense of physical well-being?

UPRIGHT

Fairness • Empathy • Charity • Reform

REVERSE

Imbalance • Unfair • Condescending • Judgment

Meaning in a Reading

UPRIGHT	REVERSE

Core Meaning

Whether it's in politics or within your parent/teacher organization at your child's school, you have the power to make a positive impact. Take advantage of your position and utilize your experience for positive reform. Employ empathy and fairness when implementing change within an organization.

Core Meaning

You're taking unfair advantage of your position of authority. Looking down your nose at people less fortunate than you carries unsavory consequences for you down the line. Rather than judging others, try walking a mile in their shoes first.

Quick-Read Meanings

LOVE

Don't be stingy with your love. Give yourself freely to your partner, and your actions will be reciprocated.

MONEY

Be generous with your money. Give where you can to those in need. Doing so will ensure balance in your own finances.

CAREER

You've been asked to monitor and distribute resources at work. Don't be intimidated by the challenge. You can make a big difference by making smart changes.

FAMILY

There is no sin in accepting charity if you need help. On the other hand, taking resources when you're fully capable of providing for yourself is ill-advised.

Quick-Read Meanings

LOVE

You're tempted to beg your lover to come back, or return to him/her. Think long and hard before you do this. Make sure there is enough value to salvage in the relationship to start again.

MONEY

Misappropriation of funds has put a lockdown on your finances. Start using better judgment with your spending habits.

CAREER

Circumstances beyond your control have the scales tipped out of balance, and not in your favor. Seek advice from a colleague with seniority or tenure.

FAMILY

You had the chance to learn about sharing resources with your family, but the lesson didn't sink in. Now you're having to learn the lesson the hard way.

THE SIX OF PENTACLES SAYS...

"It's important to know there are more resources available to you than just the standard outlets. Conventional methods of gain like bank loans or getting a second job might be counterproductive. Be aware of how you can make a positive impact on your community. Remember the law of giving and receiving which dictates that the more compassionately you contribute, the richer rewards you reap."

SEVEN OF PENTACLES

You know that old saying, "If you want it done right, do it yourself"? That phrase is particularly meaningful to you. Relying too often upon other people for your well-being isn't working for you. The only way you can satisfy your needs is through your own actions. You find freedom in personal responsibility. You take pride in your work and your ability to better your circumstances. You're learning new ways to provide for yourself, and it feels good.

When contemplating the meaning of The Seven of Pentacles, ask yourself:

How can I savor my hard work more?

Am I too self-reliant?

Do I rely on others too much or often?

How can I take more pride in my accomplishments?

Is it time to take a break?

UPRIGHT

Self-reliance • Reassessing • Provision • Reward

REVERSE

Stubborn • Failure • Inflexible • Untrusting

Meaning in a Reading

UPRIGHT	REVERSE

Core Meaning

You invested time, money, and hard work into making a better life for yourself. Be sure to take occasional breaks in your work to appreciate your progress. It's also wise to occasionally check your plans and goals to confirm you're on track.

Core Meaning

No man (or woman) is an island. You can't do everything by yourself. Your hard work is admirable, but it's time to realize you can't do it alone. Consider recruiting help, delegating, and relying on others occasionally.

Quick-Read Meanings

LOVE

You may be feeling like you need to take a break from love. Focus on yourself. Your well-being should be your top priority right now.

MONEY

Your cash flow is on the upswing. This is a good time to tweak good investments for even better returns.

CAREER

It's time to reassess. You invested extraordinary time and labor in your career; now you're in a position to forge your own path. You just need to be clear about the next direction you want to take.

FAMILY

Providing for your family pays off. Maybe it felt like a thankless job at times, but you're going to see the fruits of your labor soon.

Quick-Read Meanings

LOVE

You conducted some business with your lover. But he/she has bailed, and now you're left holding the bag. Cut your losses and do your best to recoup.

MONEY

Being stubborn and inflexible with your money has you stuck in a mindset that isn't serving you. You've become mistrusting and jaded.

CAREER

You've amassed much success and made a strong reputation for yourself. However, you're so far on top that you feel you're the only one who can do anything right. Get an ego check. You still need teamwork to succeed.

FAMILY

Check your attitude. Are you playing the martyr? Shouldering all the responsibilities and then making everybody feel guilty for not contributing isn't a healthy way to run a family.

 THE SEVEN OF PENTACLES SAYS...

"Congratulations! You employed smart methods to get positive results. Your hard work and efforts are starting to show promise. Be sure to stand back and appreciate what your hard work has produced. Enjoy this time of prosperity and productivity. Celebrate your victories. You should also plan your next move before diving back into work."

EIGHT OF PENTACLES

The Eight of Pentacles is about learning new skills, honing your craft, and hammering out details of your life. It's likely you are already good at what you do, but you have a chance to be even better. Go back to school to improve your trade. Also consider directing your craft to help your community.

When contemplating the meaning of The Eight of Pentacles, ask yourself:

Is it time to get more training?

Am I working too hard?

How can I balance my artistic vision with practical action?

Am I proud of my creation?

How can I take more pleasure from my work?

UPRIGHT

Focus • Creativity • Industry • Satisfaction

REVERSE

Obsessed • Eccentric • Reclusive • Lost

Meaning in a Reading

UPRIGHT	REVERSE

Core Meaning

Taking pride and satisfaction from a job well done is a great thrill. You are experiencing high reward from mastering a new skill. Rather than just hammering out a living, there is richness to your vocation because devotion and love for your craft are top priority.

Core Meaning

You're going through a "tortured artist" phase. You are so consumed with your work and/or art that you're ignoring everything else. People are labeling you as an eccentric because you've lost focus on the real world.

Quick-Read Meanings

LOVE

If it feels like you're beating your head against a wall to get your point across, stop it. Your partner doesn't need to be force-fed the issue.

MONEY

You're going to have to focus and get your hands dirty to accumulate the kind of wealth you're dreaming of. Time to put imagination into reality and get to work.

CAREER

Friends and family are showing interest in your hobbies. Whether cooking, photography, or woodwork, your recreational crafts are gaining attention. Consider selling your artistic creations.

FAMILY

It's time to reassess how things work at your house. You may find it more cost-effective to quit your job and stay home with the family. Talk over big changes with your partner, and see what works best.

Quick-Read Meanings

LOVE

Feelings of unworthiness have you withdrawing from partnership and love. Pull back and reassess your feelings, but don't become a hermit.

MONEY

Making money holds no interest for you. You place more value on vision, creativity, and ideals. Your focus is admirable, but don't get into the "starving artist" mindset.

CAREER

You presented some radical ideas at work, and they met with disapproval. Just because others naysay your proposals doesn't mean you're wrong. However, try to objectively see if their opinions have any merit.

FAMILY

Long hours at the office makes you a stranger at home. Your determination to provide for your family is commendable, but not at the expense of losing connection with those who need you.

THE EIGHT OF PENTACLES SAYS...

"Don't be afraid to hone your skills and branch out. Take your creations out into the world and see what happens. This implies risk because you love what you do, and might feel fear about the opinions of others. Remember: you are a gift to the world. If you don't share yourself, then you can't be a blessing to others."

NINE OF PENTACLES

The Nine of Pentacles suggests taking a vacation, exploring the world, and enjoying the finer things in life. You may feel a strong desire to hunt down new experiences. This card encourages this, and confirms now is a good time to spread your wings and take flight into new vistas. Whether you're curious to explore a new winery or take a trip to Europe, your travels will be full of promise.

When contemplating the meaning of The Nine of Pentacles, ask yourself:

Am I overindulging?

Is it time to enjoy life more?

Should I take a break, explore the world, and start a new adventure?

What am I hunting for, and how do I get it?

How can I most enjoy the beauty around me?

UPRIGHT

Travel • Exploration • Indulgence • Refinement

REVERSE

Hedonism • Overindulgence • Materialism • Illness

Meaning in a Reading

UPRIGHT	REVERSE

Core Meaning

If your life has been "ho-hum" lately, it's time to step into a new dimension. You need to change the scenery, try new things, and experience a side of life you've been missing. Meeting new people will inspire you. Learning about different cultures will ignite your creativity. Enjoy the finer things life has to offer.

Core Meaning

You've got a taste of the high life, and you like it. In fact, you like it so much you are overindulging. Treating yourself to finery isn't a problem unless you overdo it and lose sight of moderation. Obsessive consumption weakens your strength, diminishes your values, and may even cause illness.

Quick-Read Meanings

LOVE

A romantic vacation promises to kindle passion with your partner. Indulge yourself and your partner in the fine pleasures of travel.

MONEY

You are enjoying a sense of security and prosperity. This is the time to relish what you have and give thanks for your good fortune.

CAREER

You've been contemplating a change of vocation. Put your feelers out and hunt down a few possibilities that will inspire you.

FAMILY

It's important to remember home is where the heart is. You may be between homes right now, but cling to your family and everything will settle down in time.

Quick-Read Meanings

LOVE

You're being tempted and lured away from your lover by the trappings of another suitor. Just remember the grass isn't necessarily greener on the other side.

MONEY

Excessive spending has you scrambling to make ends meet. What's worse, you've been hit with a few unplanned expenses. Now is the time to cinch your belt.

CAREER

You've been knocked out of commission for awhile. Returning to work, you find the scenery has changed. Values you admired in the workforce now seem irrelevant. Keep your own inner balance as best you can.

FAMILY

Instant gratification and materialistic demands have warped your family values. Stop indulging everybody and stop buying them every little desire.

THE NINE OF PENTACLES SAYS...

"Life is good and you're experiencing a time of rich enjoyment. That doesn't mean you have to be swimming in pearls and champagne to enjoy luxury. Sometimes the simplest pleasures are more valuable than gold; for example, laughter from your loved ones, the sunshine caressing your skin, or enjoying bird song. Indulge your senses and explore the world around you."

TEN OF PENTACLES

You are living the ideal life. Health, wealth, and a loving family provide you great joy and satisfaction. You have achieved much over time, and you are now able to enjoy it. You finally obtained your goals. Continue to seek wisdom and maintain balance. Homeostasis is an ongoing effort.

When contemplating the meaning of The Ten of Pentacles, ask yourself:

What are some ways I can sustain my current joy and harmony?

How can I lay the groundwork for a better home life?

Am I being loyal to my family?

Am I adequately providing for the elderly and children in my life?

UPRIGHT

Achievement • Satisfaction • Wisdom • Family

REVERSE

Gambling • Judgment • Burdens • Loss

Meaning in a Reading

UPRIGHT	REVERSE

Core Meaning

Your perfect dream might not be a house with a picket fence and 2.5 kids with a station wagon in the garage; but if it is, then that dream is becoming a reality. If you have a different idea of a flawless life, then be prepared to see that vision become crystal clear.

Core Meaning

Family needs are taxing. You're having difficulty taking care of all the details at home. Children and/or aging family members are burdensome. Finances are rocky, and you're struggling to make ends meet. You feel you're doing your best to juggle everything, but others are judging you unfairly.

Quick-Read Meanings

LOVE

Relish a time of harmony and balance in your love relationship. You are equally yoked, and sharing responsibilities in the partnership offers great satisfaction.

MONEY

It feels good to be able to provide monetary stability to your family. Your finances are sound enough to support an aging parent or extended family member.

CAREER

You might be considering retirement. Now is a good time to bank on the security you've established. If you're not ready for retirement, consider implementing a day-care center at work or volunteering with the elderly.

FAMILY

An aging parent might need help, and you might be thinking of moving him/her into your home. The timing for this is ideal. If not, this is the time to rededicate yourself to family matters and core values.

Quick-Read Meanings

LOVE

There's a big elephant standing between you and your lover. An obvious issue needs to be addressed, but you're both ignoring it.

MONEY

A reliable source of income is in threat of going belly up. Find other sources of money to compensate.

CAREER

You want to make a change, but it threatens security, retirement, and benefits. People close to you are advising against it, too.

FAMILY

Dealing with illness in the family has you stressed and lacking energy. Extended family might be able to help.

THE TEN OF PENTACLES SAYS...

"There is no perfect family, but you have a chance to attain a close facsimile with your home life. After grinding out your goals, you have achieved a healthy balance between home, family, and monetary stability. Spend quality time with your elders and those you respect. They offer golden advice. Spend time with children and make precious memories with them."

PAGE OF **PENTACLES.**

PAGE OF PENTACLES

Are you ready to follow your higher calling? You are being tasked with serving others, and it is a great honor. Heeding the call to service will lead to satisfaction for yourself and others. If accepting new challenges makes you uncomfortable, don't worry—you have a marvelous support group cheering you on.

When contemplating the meaning of The Page of Pentacles, ask yourself:

Am I ready to receive my highest honor?

Am I willing to travel in order to excel?

How can I offer better service to others?

How can I avoid childish reactions and maturely accept responsibility?

UPRIGHT

Support • Service • Travel • Industry

REVERSE

Resentment • Childish • Ignorance • Self-involved

Meaning in a Reading

UPRIGHT	REVERSE

Core Meaning

You're met with an opportunity you never expected. This path will lead to a good way of life, satisfaction, and serenity. Expect "hands on" training, or working with your hands to provide a quality service to others. You are having to tend to the needs of others, but you have support. Travel to meet challenges is likely.

Core Meaning

Someone is an adult, but is acting like a two year old. If this is you, grow up and accept responsibility. If it's someone you know, it's time to employ tough love. Calmly explain that this selfish behavior can't continue without unsavory consequences.

Quick-Read Meanings

LOVE

Your partner is extending a peace offering or presenting you with a gift. This will be something of lasting substance.

MONEY

Take the challenge you've received regarding a financial investment. It will take nurturing, but it will succeed under your supervision and care.

CAREER

News of a promotion is cycling through the work place. Commuting or traveling to a new location may be required to get a job done.

FAMILY

Your family is on solid ground and ready to take on a new responsibility. This may be a new addition to the family or participating in a challenge with all members involved.

Quick-Read Meanings

LOVE

Somebody didn't get his/her way. Foot-stomping and pouting isn't likely to help. Selfish motives are causing the blush of your love to fade.

MONEY

Greed and laziness are not ideal bedfellows. Switch your attitude to generosity and hard work before your finances take a nosedive.

CAREER

Resenting your fellow co-workers for their success is foolish and juvenile. Instead, try cheering others on for their accomplishments.

FAMILY

Stop the whining! Family members are cranky because they're being asked to chip in when they'd rather watch TV or play video games. It's time to shape up or ship out.

THE PAGE OF PENTACLES SAYS...

"Family and social conditions are favorable for your best success. You have a phenomenal support group that will help you climb the mountain of challenge you are facing. Be willing to travel (perhaps long distances) to give the world your greatest gifts. You may be comfortable where you are, but pushing yourself will lead to greater satisfaction."

KNIGHT OF **PENTACLES**

Every inch of you wants to push forward, spring into action, and take charge. Nevertheless, you have the sense this isn't the best idea. Listen to your intuition. A fact-finding mission needs to be launched before moving ahead.

When contemplating the meaning of The Knight of Pentacles, ask yourself:

Do I have all the details before I go forward?

Am I properly equipped before taking action?

How can I be more thoughtful in this situation?

Who or what needs my protection and am I providing it?

What's the simplest solution?

UPRIGHT

Thoughtful • Preparedness • Protection • Simplicity

REVERSE

Idle • Apathy • Careless • Unobservant

118

Meaning in a Reading

UPRIGHT	REVERSE

Core Meaning

You're met with an opportunity you never expected. This path will lead to a good way of life, satisfaction, and serenity. Expect "hands on" training, or working with your hands to provide a quality service to others. You are having to tend to the needs of others, but you have support. Travel to meet challenges is likely.

Core Meaning

In light of recent events, you decided the best course of action is taking none at all. It seems you've lost the spring in your step, and your zest for life is lacking. You've ceased to care about things that are important. Even your appearance and finances have fallen short of previous standards.

Quick-Read Meanings

LOVE

Your partner wants to move forward in your relationship, maybe even propose marriage. You, on the other hand, would be best served to think before accepting.

MONEY

Put your money toward a noble quest. Invest in social or civic groups. Do your research first, and determine the best way to make your money work for the community.

CAREER

You feel like the last warrior standing in a battlefield of reductions, cutbacks, and layoffs. Play your cards right and you can benefit greatly—even in current calamity.

FAMILY

You're having to protect your stance on an issue of value or money. Gird yourself. Be resolute. Stand firm and don't cave into petty requests.

Quick-Read Meanings

LOVE

Your partner has given up on you, and it's punched a hole in your world. Rather than viewing it as an end to your love life, think of it as temporarily stalled.

MONEY

If money flowed from faucets, yours would be blocked by emotional calcification. Cleaning out the sediment of your bad attitude will prompt your finances to get flowing again.

CAREER

Your industry is stagnant right now. This uninspired condition makes you lethargic and apathetic. Pay attention to opportunities outside your career.

FAMILY

A family member is being careless with his/her responsibilities. He/she is falling short of your expectations. Have a talk. There may be a valid reason.

THE KNIGHT OF PENTACLES SAYS...

"You are on the precipice of a great quest. You're prepared and qualified to take the challenge. Starting this venture will lead you to new perception and material gains. There's only one catch. You're going to have to be absolutely positive you have all the information before pursuing your adventure. Do research, be thoughtful, and protect your assets before taking the first step."

KNIGHT OF PENTACLES

QUEEN OF PENTACLES.

QUEEN OF PENTACLES

You are more in tune with your feminine, mothering side than ever before. You are enjoying the beauty around you. You are sensitive to your environment and the needs of others. You count your blessings, give thanks, and give to your family. You feel satisfied because the prosperity you enjoy is a direct result of the hard work and sacrifices you have made.

When contemplating the meaning of The Queen of Pentacles, ask yourself:

How can I savor the simple pleasures in my life?

Am I grateful for my family, home, and resources?

Can I be more nurturing and supporting in my relationships?

Am I being more sensitive to the needs of others?

UPRIGHT

Sensitivity • Pleasure • Contentment • Nurturing

REVERSE

Superficial • Guilt • Overburdened • Martyrdom • Deceit

Meaning in a Reading

UPRIGHT	REVERSE

Core Meaning

Nurturing things of value in your life will give you a sense of intense gratification and pleasure. You can achieve this satisfaction by simply tending to a houseplant or taking a more active maternal role in your family or community. Simple gestures go a long way. Even the smallest kindnesses you extend will reap big results.

Core Meaning

These days, the common meaning of *martyr* is someone who exaggerates pain or suffering in order to gain sympathy and attention. Does this ring a bell for you? Everyone gets overburdened and stressed out, but it's what we do about it that counts. Don't use your pain to inflict guilt on others.

Quick-Read Meanings

LOVE

The most important love affair you can have right now is the one with yourself. Take time to appreciate and comfort yourself.

MONEY

Take a long, thoughtful look at your finances. You may find you can rely on your own resources to meet your needs. For example, start a garden for produce instead of paying for it at the market.

CAREER

Placement in a supervisory role offers a lot of potential to make a difference in the lives you influence. Don't just be a boss; be a mentor.

FAMILY

Your family blooms under your tender, loving care. Take time to smell the roses with your loved ones. Take a nature hike and share simple pleasures together.

Quick-Read Meanings

LOVE

Giving your lover the cold shoulder is neither fair nor mature. You may have reason, but there are better ways to express dissatisfaction with your mate.

MONEY

Using deceit or manipulation for monetary gain might seem appealing to you. Think twice before you employ trickery to get what you want.

CAREER

You had an amazing chance to make an impact, but instead you let your ego get in the way. Curtail superficial behavior and add value to the workplace. Doing so will enhance your career.

FAMILY

A strong female, such as a mother, uses guilt to get results. This tactic is hurtful and damaging. Recognize the guilt trips, and don't allow them to make you stumble.

THE QUEEN OF PENTACLES SAYS...

"You are sitting pretty in a peaceful place. You learned a few lessons the hard way, but now you see the value in the struggle. You know life is like a garden. You have to cultivate and nurture it in order to savor the beauty. Your tender compassion allows love to grow."

QUEEN OF PENTACLES

KING OF PENTACLES

The King of Pentacles represents masculinity and all its powerful implications. In a reading, this card suggests you use strength and strategy to establish security. You acquired wealth, territory, and status. You take pride in your kingdom (family and social circles). You are a mentor, and people look to you for advice. You are also very protective, and willing to fiercely defend your acquisitions.

When contemplating the meaning of The King of Pentacles, ask yourself:

Am I being mature with my resources?

How can I enhance my confidence without coming across as arrogant?

Am I a good leader and mentor?

How can I exhibit strength and influence without letting my ego get in the way?

UPRIGHT

Confidence • Strength • Charisma • Strategy

REVERSE

Chauvinism • Belligerence • Abusive • Overcompensating

Meaning in a Reading

UPRIGHT	REVERSE

Core Meaning

Power, prestige, and influence are yours to enjoy. You have a lot of sway with your colleagues and you're able to pull strings to get things done in your world. Rather than shirk responsibilities, you relish them. You take pride in exerting your power and control. You relish challenges because you know you can conquer and overcome.

Core Meaning

You are in a position of power. Unfortunately, you're tempted to abuse this power and wield it over others. You definitely have advantages, but that doesn't give you the right to feel superior. Others may think you are overcompensating for emotional lack.

Quick-Read Meanings

LOVE

You love the strength and independence in your mate. However, sometimes those qualities are overwhelming. Avoid power struggles in the relationship. Employ strategy and consideration to maintain balance.

MONEY

Your finances are at the forefront of your attention. You know you can get ahead if you stick to your plan. Others are asking you for financial advice.

CAREER

You are putting your foot down at work. Taking a firm stand will earn you respect and get results.

FAMILY

You are a linchpin within the family. You are a natural mentor, and your loved ones draw close for your stability and strength.

Quick-Read Meanings

LOVE

Don't let your mate rule over you. Likewise, don't try to control your partner. Being stubborn is causing a wedge between you and your loved one.

MONEY

Do you think having money makes you better than everyone else? Think again. That attitude is alienating and crippling to you and others.

CAREER

You may have good reason to feel elite, but boasting about it at work isn't doing much to advance your career. Give humility a try.

FAMILY

The "my way or the highway" approach doesn't work. Rules are necessary for a functional family life, but you can implement them without cramming them down the family's throat.

THE KING OF PENTACLES SAYS...

"You have a lot to manage and it's not easy to keep your finger on the pulse of everything. Luckily, you are well seasoned, mature, and prepared for anything. The only challenge you have in life is balancing your power and strength with humility. It's natural to boast about your accomplishments. Nevertheless, a good leader is one who knows his/her position of power but doesn't have to flaunt it."

KING OF PENTACLES

THE SUIT OF SWORDS

ACE OF SWORDS.

ACE OF SWORDS

You have a sharp mental ability to discern your needs and goals. This is the time for focus on new opportunities and directions. A bright idea has occurred to you. Take initiative to pursue it.

When contemplating the meaning of The Ace of Swords, ask yourself:

How can I maintain mental focus?

Am I letting other people take advantage of me?

How can I take more initiative?

What is my concept of god, and is it serving me?

UPRIGHT

Initiative • Beginning • Clarity • Focus

REVERSE

Boredom • Backward • Insecurity • Shyness

Meaning in a Reading

UPRIGHT	REVERSE

Core Meaning

Consider cutting away the old and implementing new ways of doing things. Outdated ways of thinking are holding you back. Your ideas and mental focus are your crowning glory. There are invisible forces that support your endeavors.

Core Meaning

Apathy and carelessness are causing a downward turn in your attitude. Your concern for yourself and others is faltering. Reverting to old habits is prohibiting your ability to move forward in life. Insecurity paralyzes you from getting out and enjoying social settings.

Quick-Read Meanings

LOVE

You deserve respect. Recognize your value, and don't settle for less than what you deserve.

MONEY

You've been cooking up a brilliant idea. Stop scribbling your plans on cocktail napkins and start putting your formulas to work in the real world.

CAREER

You feel the need to take action at work. You're tempted to use brute force to create change, but mental strategy is a better tactic.

FAMILY

Be clear about the needs of your family members. There are reasons others are acting out in negative ways. Open smart dialogue and cut through the fog to get to the bottom of conflict.

Quick-Read Meanings

LOVE

Your partner made a move that offended you. This action gives you pause about the future of your relationship. Consider talking to a pastor or relationship counselor for perspective.

MONEY

Your career is moving backward and you feel isolated. Not all the details are clear. Your position is frozen right now.

CAREER

You may have good reason to feel elite, but boasting about it at work isn't doing much to advance your career. Give humility a try.

FAMILY

A family member stabbed you in the back, causing you to withdraw from the world. Seek spiritual guidance and try to forgive.

 THE ACE OF SWORDS SAYS...

"Your point of focus is key. What happens within you is a direct reflection of what happens outside of you. Your thoughts and emotions directly influence what happens in your world. Be clear about what you want. Being focused about positive objectives will serve you well."

ACE OF SWORDS

TWO OF SWORDS

You are in a unique place in life. You are on solid ground while the world around you seems chaotic and foreign. You are self-invested. Meditation, spirituality, and prayer are highly important to you. You experience calm, peace, and tranquility in spite of an unknown future. You are not allowing distractions to knock you off your foundation.

When contemplating the meaning of The Two of Swords, ask yourself:

How can I trust my intuition more?

How can I be more calm and centered?

How can I establish serenity and self-assurance?

How can I stop forcing things and just trust in timing more?

UPRIGHT

Intuition • Meditation • Calm • Self-assurance

REVERSE

Conflicted • Overemotional • Impatience • Blind • Fear

Meaning in a Reading

UPRIGHT	REVERSE

Core Meaning

You are impervious to problems. You know you have the intelligence and strength to handle what comes your way. You have no need to prove yourself. You are at the crossroads between two choices, but you should not feel pressured to act right now.

Core Meaning

Fear of the unknown is paralyzing. Your inability to make a decision makes you fearful and anxious. You are blinded by your own emotions and cannot be objective. Conflict and impatience keep you edgy and irritable.

Quick-Read Meanings

LOVE

Follow your intuition. You may not have all the details, but being calm and following your heart will serve you.

MONEY

The best action is inaction. You have two financial opportunities at your feet. Don't jump to conclusions or make a choice because you feel pressured. You have plenty of time to decide.

CAREER

There is a big promotion looming in the distance. Stay calm and self-assured. Your ship will come in, but you have to remain composed. Don't fight for advancement, it will come to you naturally.

FAMILY

You have to focus on yourself and your own needs. Meditate, exercise, read—do things that honor yourself and put you in a place of serenity. This will pay off for you and your family.

Quick-Read Meanings

LOVE

Stop ignoring the problems. Your relationship may be easy, but that doesn't mean it's healthy.

MONEY

You detect financial unrest. Instead of taking a calm, practical approach, you are worrying and obsessing. Ignoring solutions and bemoaning the problem only makes it worse.

CAREER

You're impatient because you're not getting results from your actions. Events have been put into motion that you are not aware of. Quit forcing the issue. Things will fall into place if you let go.

FAMILY

A family member is trying to play two sides. This might be children manipulating both parents, or perhaps power plays in custody issues. Try to remain calm and follow your intuition.

THE TWO OF SWORDS SAYS...

"It's true that taking action is one way to see results. But in this instance, you need to settle yourself into a peaceful place and realize no action is required of you at this time. If you stay calm and centered, you will see amazing results. Don't let your self-assurance be swayed by external influence or distractions. Inner strength is the way to outer stability."

TWO OF SWORDS

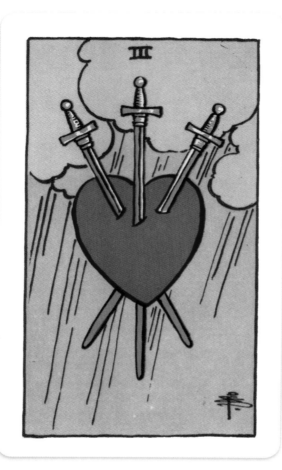

THREE OF SWORDS

There are piercing issues at the heart of your awareness. Things that matter most to you feel threatened. You may experience close friends or family stabbing you in the back. There may be a love triangle you have to address. Health issues may be at the forefront. Consider a healthy-heart check up.

When contemplating the meaning of The Three of Swords, ask yourself:

How can I deal with betrayal in a healthy manner?

What were the warning signs, and why didn't I see them?

How can I nurture my renewed faith and trust?

Is it time to get a health check up?

UPRIGHT

Conflict • Pain • Warning • Deception

REVERSE

Passionate • Faith • Precision • Inspection

Meaning in a Reading

UPRIGHT	REVERSE

Core Meaning

Hurt feelings come from the actions of others against you. This shouldn't come as a surprise; you had warnings prior to the event. Feelings of resentment may tempt you or loved ones to hold a grudge. A time of grief and shedding tears will cleanse your soul.

Core Meaning

Where your perception was cloudy before, now you are seeing your life with clear vision. Not everything is perfect, but you have the strength to face your challenges head on.

Quick-Read Meanings

LOVE

A love triangle threatens your harmony. Cut through doubt and find the facts if you suspect infidelity.

MONEY

Instead of just putting a bandage to your monetary wounds, employ long-lasting solutions that can weather any storm.

CAREER

You've got competition. Someone is gunning for your position, and it's putting you on pins and needles. Steel yourself for the worst, but the results might not be as painful as you think.

FAMILY

Get your family checked for health and wellness. Don't allow misunderstanding or betrayals to form a bitter grudge in your heart.

Quick-Read Meanings

LOVE

After a painful separation you are reunited. Trepidation and reestablishing trust are at the heart of the relationship.

MONEY

You heeded warning signs about threats to your finances. Your attempts to avoid money problems were effective, and you are establishing balance.

CAREER

You are passionate about your career. So much so that your zest for work sometimes blinds you from everything else. Make sure your heart has enough room for other healthy interests.

FAMILY

After close inspection, certain truths are surfacing within the family. This may deal with health issues that were hidden from you, or perhaps hidden addictions. You're going to have to deal with these issues head on.

THREE OF SWORDS

THE THREE OF SWORDS SAYS...

"Nobody likes his/her heart broken, but sometimes it's unavoidable. It's important to identify the warning signs of trouble. If you didn't see a heartbreak coming, question why you chose to ignore the signs. Lean upon faith and spiritual devotion to sustain your heart."

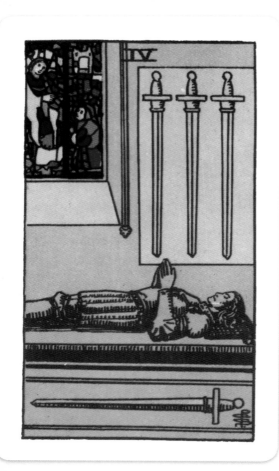

FOUR OF SWORDS

You need a break. You've known this for awhile, but you're convinced there isn't enough time for rest in your busy schedule. Think again. This card assures that spending time in quiet meditation will reap more rewards than any action could ever produce. This card advises you to depend on your subconscious mind and your spiritual guidance to help you see clarity.

When contemplating the meaning of The Four of Swords, ask yourself:

Should I sleep on the issue rather than taking action?

How can I become more calm and centered?

How can I rely more on spiritual wisdom?

What facts am I ignoring and why?

UPRIGHT

Contemplation • Meditation • Inner focus • Spirituality

REVERSE

Refusal • Forced • Ignoring • Resentment

Meaning in a Reading

UPRIGHT	REVERSE

Core Meaning

You must find a way to stabilize your inner turmoil through serene, inner focus. There is a fundamental issue you need to address. Consider solving this issue in the invisible, spiritual realms first. Quietly contemplate solutions in the solace of your heart.

Core Meaning

A strong conviction to change your ways and see the light of reason is upon you. For various reasons, you are ignoring the chance to live better. You feel forced to stay in your old life. This causes frustration and resentment. Refusing to grow and make better choices keeps you powerless.

Quick-Read Meanings

LOVE

It's time to take a break in the relationship. There is a bone of contention between you and your partner that requires your attention. There are a few other issues, but you can overlook them.

MONEY

Recover your finances by recovering your mental stability. Sit out of the money-making game for a bit.

CAREER

You can't be touched by competition or naysayers. You exude silent confidence and poise in your work. Your wisdom and experience speaks for itself. You don't have to convince anybody.

FAMILY

Keeping the household in order takes a lot of your energy. If you don't get some rest, you're going to burn out. Enforce daily quiet time. Your family will understand.

Quick-Read Meanings

LOVE

You're refusing to see the obvious. Be honest with yourself and accept the truth. Confronting the problem may be unsavory, but deluding yourself will be much more painful.

MONEY

You're forced to put a hold on all your financial plans. Money will flow again, but you need to accept this time of inaction.

CAREER

A vital point of interest has popped up on your radar. This detail is keeping you from moving forward. Don't resent the circumstances. Accept the facts and find a way to work around them.

FAMILY

You're in pain and you should talk about it. You're being stubborn and not sharing because you don't want your family to take pity.

FOUR OF SWORDS

 ## THE FOUR OF SWORDS SAYS...

"It's simple. Being tired is a sign you need rest. Don't feel guilty about stepping out of the action for awhile. You will perform better and think more clearly if you do. Pay attention to your dreams at night. They may offer vital insights. Employ more meditation and prayer in your daily life. Implementing rest and quiet introspection will pay off more than action."

FIVE OF SWORDS

There is foul play afoot. You've taken rash action because you badly wanted someone or something. You didn't consider how your actions might hurt others' feelings. You forced an issue or behaved rudely. You are so driven by your own wants, you aren't thinking clearly.

When contemplating the meaning of The Five of Swords, ask yourself:

Do I always have to be right? Why?

How can I get what I want without hurting others?

Is my sense of entitlement justified?

How can I employ sharing and forgiveness?

Do I resolve disagreements in a healthy way?

UPRIGHT

Trickery • Selfishness • Disagreement • Entitlement

REVERSE

Resolution • Understanding • Realization • Forgiveness

Meaning in a Reading

UPRIGHT	REVERSE

Core Meaning

You feel like you are entitled to have what you want. Friends and loved ones try to reason with you, but you're not listening. You are convinced you know all the answers and deserve the best. That may be true, but you're going about getting your needs met in the wrong way.

Core Meaning

There is no shortage of disagreements in your life, but you choose to take the high road and forgive others. Your motivations in the past have been questionable, but you've come to realize what's most important to you. You will experience reunions and a meeting of the minds.

Quick-Read Meanings

LOVE

Someone is getting used in the relationship. You or your lover are taking more than giving. Realizing this causes a rift. Be fair in the relationship.

MONEY

Your sense of entitlement is making you greedy. Don't gloat over financial victories. Consider being more charitable.

CAREER

You may deserve advancement in your job, but being boastful makes your superiors think twice about giving you a chance for promotion.

FAMILY

Bargaining with your family to get them to do what you want might be effective, but it's unhealthy. Find fair ways to negotiate mutual satisfaction within the home.

Quick-Read Meanings

LOVE

Expect a reconciliation with your partner. Mutual respect and admiration brings the two of you back together with new understanding.

MONEY

You finally understand that making money isn't a bad thing. You know that money can be a positive influence to you and others in your life.

CAREER

After a time of confusion and disagreements, you will experience understanding in the workplace now. You will be adept at solving problems for the good of the whole.

FAMILY

Conflict of opinions are now dissolved. You and your family have reached an agreement. The family bands together to share resources.

THE FIVE OF SWORDS SAYS...

"You may be the best—and people may look up to you—but gloating about it isn't winning you any friends. People need you, but you need them just as much. Don't let your ego cloud your judgment and make you crazy. Sharing your knowledge and resources does not diminish your power."

FIVE OF SWORDS

SIX OF SWORDS

Whether out of fear or necessity, you feel you must flee from a bad situation. You are seeking guidance from someone you trust. You have been advised to cut your losses and leave with what little value and dignity you have left. The path you take is difficult and unstable. You are not alone; you will have the support you need to make this transition.

When contemplating the meaning of The Six of Swords, ask yourself:

Is it time for me to move on?

What am I willing to do to protect my family and/or assets?

Who can I trust and am I listening to their advice?

How can I better navigate through emotional turbulence?

UPRIGHT

Fleeing • Relocation • Protection • Self-improvement

REVERSE

Delay • Unwillingness • Procrastination • Unbalanced

Meaning in a Reading

UPRIGHT	REVERSE

Core Meaning

You are finally taking action to improve your situation. You may have been forced to move out of poverty, sickness, or depression. You have a chance to move into a better place for yourself and your family. Listen to advice from someone with skill and experience. You are supported in your endeavors.

Core Meaning

You know your circumstances are untenable and unhealthy, but you feel powerless or just don't have the energy to navigate out of the bad situations. Setbacks and broken promises are painful to your spirit; you feel alone and unable to protect your assets.

Quick-Read Meanings

LOVE

You are leaving a relationship. This is painful, and there is a degree of shame involved. Take hope from the fact that you are moving out of a bad time into a better life.

MONEY

Save what you can, and pull the plug on other investments. Don't live in the past to save your future.

CAREER

You are asked to carry out an important duty. The responsibility is close to your heart. You accept the challenge, and take your performance personally.

FAMILY

There may be abuse within the family which forces you to move to better conditions. You may find yourself a single parent fending for yourself and your child. Seek support from trusted sources.

Quick-Read Meanings

LOVE

Your partner is controlling and manipulative. You're making excuses and are unwilling to help yourself out of an unbalanced partnership.

MONEY

The income you are expecting is delayed. Don't give up hope. Motions behind the scenes are taking place, it's just taking awhile to get payment to you.

CAREER

You are procrastinating at work, and people are starting to notice. For some reason, you don't feel deserving of promotion. Try to avoid self-sabotage.

FAMILY

You want to run away from your family because there is a gross imbalance within the home. Instead of being anxious to leave, be willing to listen, reconcile, and mend fences.

THE SIX OF SWORDS SAYS...

Sometimes the only way to be a better person is to remove yourself from an unhealthy situation. Take an inventory of the emotional, mental, and physical needs of yourself and your loved ones. If it feels there is no choice but to sever ties and flee, then don't ignore that instinct. Don't stay in a bad spot just because you fear the unknown or because you are trying to keep your pride intact."

SIX OF SWORDS

SEVEN OF SWORDS

Pulling this card often means you are getting away with something. You have valuable information and resources, but you're not sharing. More accurately, you want to take your knowledge and run with it. You may feel a sense of glee and liberation in knowing you have power over others. You know things others don't, and you like that feeling of superiority.

When contemplating the meaning of The Seven of Swords, ask yourself:

Am I being honest with others and myself?

What am I running away from? Why?

What am I trying to get away with?

Am I sharing my resources?

Am I turning my back on important values or people?

UPRIGHT

Escape • Inconsiderate • Irresponsibility • Temporary

REVERSE

Responsibility • Cessation • Reformation • Adjusting

Meaning in a Reading

UPRIGHT	REVERSE

UPRIGHT

Core Meaning

You have a chance to make a difference, but you are unwilling to commit. You have wild oats to sew, and settling down is the last thing on your mind. You have plenty of options and resources, but you don't want to share with others. Enjoy this lifestyle for the moment; it won't last.

Quick-Read Meanings

LOVE

You are toying with your partner's emotions. Your mate wants you to commit, but you're unwilling or incapable. Stop stringing your partner along.

MONEY

Newfound finances allow you to do some travel and gain new experiences. Don't squander your earnings in one place; your monetary increase might be temporary. Plant some seeds to invest in your future.

CAREER

Everybody at work is a clown, and you seem to be the ring master. It's time to sober up and get serious. You have a chance to make a real difference. Don't ditch responsibility in favor of temporary pursuits.

FAMILY

Whether relocating or taking an extended trip, your family is on the move. Pay attention to details while you are in transit. Make sure you don't leave something important behind.

REVERSE

Core Meaning

Personal mistakes you made are coming to your attention. You feel compelled to take responsibility and face the music for your actions. Lessons learned allow you to stop bad habits and take better action. You want to right your wrongs and make amends.

Quick-Read Meanings

LOVE

You find yourself looking into the past. Your relationship was different in the beginning and you want to find a way to recapture what's been lost.

MONEY

A revelation about money has you stopped in your tracks. You make better choices about giving and receiving. You are more considerate about finances.

CAREER

Your colleagues laughed at a proposal and refused to get involved. You, on the other hand, are convinced there is merit to the project. You are willing to commit and risk it all to see the idea into reality.

FAMILY

You're trying to reform the behavior of a family member. This may mean calling an intervention. While you're trying to adjust his/her attitude, consider your own attitude as well.

THE SEVEN OF SWORDS SAYS...

"Peter Pan is the boy who refused to grow up. You can relate to that right now. Although your youthful enthusiasm is charming to many people, it is distasteful to others. You are getting pressure to be more mature and take responsibility. Your behavior might be a form of escape. There is a time and place for being free. Recognize the need for appropriate behavior."

EIGHT OF SWORDS

You set your sights high, but circumstances didn't live up to your expectations. The disappointment paralyzed you and you feel victimized. You are ignoring other opportunities. Your negative attitude is preventing you from taking action. Constant worry and nagging thoughts keep you feeling powerless.

When contemplating the meaning of The Eight of Swords, ask yourself:

- How can I avoid feeling like a victim?
- How can I work with disappointment rather than let it defeat me?
- How can I get my power and control back?
- Have I given up on my ideals and goals?

UPRIGHT

Paralyzed • Inaction • Disappointment • Self-pity

REVERSE

Seriousness • Integrity • Resolution • Discovery

140

Meaning in a Reading

UPRIGHT	REVERSE

Core Meaning

You are having a tough time coping with challenges. You established a plan, but it fell through. You feel your efforts are futile. You would rather shut down and withdraw into yourself than deal with problems. You can't see a solution amidst so many difficulties.

Core Meaning

You must stand resolute about an issue you're struggling with. It is vital to remain strong and focused. Keep your ideals and goals clear in your vision for the future. Be firm about who you are and what you want. Don't buckle under pressure, and don't be distracted.

Quick-Read Meanings

LOVE

You are dealing with major disappointment in the relationship. You may be the victim, but self-pity will not improve the situation.

MONEY

All your money is tied up in something big. Perhaps your house is a money pit or a venture is sucking your finances like quick sand. The more you struggle, the worse it will get.

CAREER

You are mired in excessive details and petty tasks. You cannot see your objective clearly because there are too many distractions.

FAMILY

You had high hopes about establishing a secure, stable home life. Don't give up on the dream just because you're experiencing setbacks.

Quick-Read Meanings

LOVE

You've been hurt in a relationship, but you are determined to heal and overcome. You will need self-love and self-honesty to move through the pain.

MONEY

While others around you are playing dirty, you insist on being a straight shooter. Keep that high-minded attitude, and you will get the financial backing you expect.

CAREER

You are a lighthouse in your industry. Others look to you for direction, clarity, and integrity. Remain a shining beacon. You are more than your function at work. You are a mentor.

FAMILY

Expect a resolution to emotional struggles you've been having within the family. Someone has been dealing with some demons. Those are about to be exorcised.

THE EIGHT OF SWORDS SAYS...

"Go within yourself for answers. Don't allow problems to overwhelm you. You may feel powerless, but that is an illusion. If you continue to experience setbacks on your way to reaching your goals, try stepping back. Rather than getting tied up in difficulties, take time to quietly reflect on solutions. You may feel like a victim of circumstances, but that attitude only makes matters worse."

NINE OF SWORDS

You are obsessing over an issue and it's causing sleepless nights. You keep working to find answers, but they are elusive. You are grieving over a loss and you fear you might lose more in the future. You cannot let go of nagging negativity and it may be causing health issues.

When contemplating the meaning of The Nine of Swords, ask yourself:

Am I paying attention to my health needs?

What are my dreams trying to tell me?

How is obsessing over things serving me?

How can I surrender my grief?

UPRIGHT

Crisis • Obsessing • Illness • Fear

REVERSE

Spirituality • Revelation • Perception • Fantasy

Meaning in a Reading

UPRIGHT	REVERSE

Core Meaning

Problems, loss, or a crisis are causing physical and/or mental decline. There may be tendencies for obsessive behavior because you are trying to reestablish control. Fear and negative thought run rampant and prohibit you from relaxing. Exhaustion causes paranoia and anxiety. You have to find a way to let go, and allow a power greater than yourself to guide you out of despair.

Core Meaning

You keep receiving signs from the universe about your future. Spirituality becomes a focus. Dreams and fantasy become a reality. You are interested in psychic sciences like astrology, palmistry, and ESP. You feel connected to the world through prayer, the healing arts, and intuitive perception. You are aligning your energy to be more attuned to the invisible nature of life.

Quick-Read Meanings

LOVE

A painful loss of love causes a deep sense of grief and isolation. Acceptance is your only hope for relief. Transform anguish into a learning experience.

MONEY

Poor financial planning has you riddled with stress. Guilt and fear cloud your judgment. Consult a financial planner for clarity and solutions.

CAREER

You are obsessing about work. Consider relaxation techniques, aroma therapy, or taking up a hobby to help you unwind.

FAMILY

You or a family member is suffering from a physical or mental decline, and obligations are piling up. Focus on health and wellness. Everything else must take a back seat.

Quick-Read Meanings

LOVE

You're repeating the same routine with your mate. Try new activities together. Consider taking a spiritual retreat together, or go on an outing to a healing spa.

MONEY

Put your money concerns to bed and focus on other interests. Use your money to expand your education or explore hobbies and recreational pursuits.

CAREER

Employ more intuition and social observation in the workplace. Consider being more compassionate and understanding toward co-workers.

FAMILY

A family that prays together stays together. No matter what your religious beliefs are, it is important to expose the family to spiritual wisdom at this time.

THE NINE OF SWORDS SAYS...

"You are experiencing a dark night of the soul, and this forces you to take a hard look at your life. Loss, fear, and guilt threaten to overtake your mind and body. You have the option to seek guidance from a higher power. Explore different ways of thought to shift your perception out of a negative groove. You have an opportunity to grow stronger through a time of crisis."

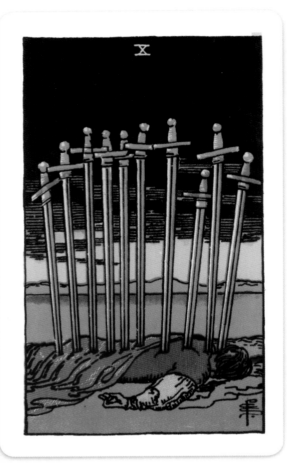

TEN OF SWORDS

Overworked and overburdened, you now have no choice but to rest. You are forced to relinquish control. You took on too much, and now you have to give up some responsibilities. You had fair warning that trouble was pending, but you kept pushing. Now you are pinned in with no option but to surrender.

When contemplating the meaning of The Ten of Swords, ask yourself:

Is it time for a health check up?

How can I surrender my problems?

Could my suffering lead to renewal?

Am I paying attention to warning signs?

UPRIGHT

Surrender • Health • Release • Pinned

REVERSE

Hope • Renewal • Acceptance • Turnaround

Meaning in a Reading

UPRIGHT	REVERSE

Core Meaning

Focus on your health. You may be dealing with back problems that need attention. Nerve damage might also be an issue. Consider chiropractic care or acupuncture to align your energy and body. Taking on too much mental, emotional, or physical burden leaves you feeling pinned down and unable to make a move. Surrendering leads to cleansing, and allows you to start anew.

Core Meaning

Life has been hard, but you are experiencing a reversal in fortune. New opportunities for growth have you feeling alive and hopeful for the first time in awhile. You are getting a new lease on life and feel a renewed sense of purpose. These inspired moments come only after you accept your limitations and surrender to the things you can't change.

Quick-Read Meanings

LOVE

You may have been stabbed in the back, but this works in your favor. You are free to discover a more rewarding, loving relationship now.

MONEY

You're down, but not out. It may seem like you are forced in a financial quagmire, but relax. A solution is on the horizon.

CAREER

You are pinned in a position that wears you down. You ache for a new opportunity and better conditions. You will have your chance soon.

FAMILY

The daily obligations of family life are getting on your last nerve. You feel pinched and stuck in a life you didn't choose. Talk to a trusted friend to unburden yourself.

Quick-Read Meanings

LOVE

You have been given a blessing to move on. This may mean getting the "ok" to start a new relationship after grieving over an old one.

MONEY

After accepting a few defeating facts about finances, you can now see an opportunity for monetary growth.

CAREER

It's been uphill for you at work, but now the hard part is over. Expect to harvest the fruit of your labor, and relax a little.

FAMILY

You received news about your family that initially shocked you. In time, you accepted the information. Reconciliation and healing are a direct result of your understanding.

THE TEN OF SWORDS SAYS...

"The best thing about being at an all-time low is that things can only go up from here. Hitting rock bottom is often the only way to access hope and start fresh. If you have nothing to lose, then you are free to move in any direction you like. You are no longer constrained or pinned down by the weight of the world."

PAGE OF SWORDS.

PAGE OF SWORDS

The Page of Swords delivers good news. You or someone you know has received information that will clarify goals and direction. You have a fantastic vantage point in life right now. You're in a perfect position to make the right choices and serve others in positive ways.

When contemplating the meaning of The Page of Swords, ask yourself:

Am I ready to accept change?

Am I aware enough to notice opportunity?

How can I embrace mental clarity?

How can I communicate more clearly?

How can I be more mindful of the needs of others?

UPRIGHT

Communication • Clarity • Change • Thoughtfulness

REVERSE

Irritable • Unwanted • Unknown • Denial

Meaning in a Reading

UPRIGHT	REVERSE

Core Meaning

The winds of change are blowing in your life. Be prepared for a new wave of inspiration and clarity. You will receive a visitor bringing news of ways you can serve yourself and others more effectively. Mental focus is sharp, and you feel the need to invest more thought in your future.

Core Meaning

Fear of the unknown puts you on the defensive. You are inflexible and emitting negative vibes. This puts you and others on edge. You are fighting unwanted influences, but in doing so you are denying good things, too.

Quick-Read Meanings

LOVE

A new relationship gives you a youthful glow. Enjoy a springtime sensation and renewal in your love life.

MONEY

You are on top of your money game. You received the right tools and data to enhance your financial standing.

CAREER

Even though you might not have all the details, you can still move forward. Keep working to implement change and positive communication in the workplace.

FAMILY

Fate will blow in a visitor, and this person is a welcome surprise. You will accept this person as one of your own family, and the change he/she imposes will be positive.

Quick-Read Meanings

LOVE

You struck out against your partner, and now the status of the relationship is unclear. Solving internal conflict will offer a chance to heal the damage done.

MONEY

You took questionable advice or got duped into investing in a poor deal. Resist the urge to lash out and take revenge. Stand on your own two feet and dig yourself out by your own intelligence.

CAREER

You feel unwanted and redundant at work. You have fears about job security. Getting angry about it will only reinforce the problems.

FAMILY

Unwanted houseguests are taxing and getting on your nerves. Recognize these visitors might need your help. Try to be a good host without allowing yourself to be taken advantage of.

PAGE OF SWORDS

THE PAGE OF SWORDS SAYS...

"Open your sails, and prepare for the wind of change to move you in a new, promising direction. Keep your mind open and your schedule clear because new people and adventures are entering your life. Keep a sense of playfulness as you communicate with others. Maintain an attitude of gratitude and service. Be ready for inspiration and thought-provoking ideas."

147

KNIGHT OF SWORDS

KNIGHT OF SWORDS.

A sharp thought has pierced your mind, and you feel you must act on it. In fact, you are compelled and driven by this idea. Nothing distracts you from running with the picture you have in your head. Your determination is admirable, but it blinds you to everything else. People question you, but you turn a blind eye to their suggestions to take things slowly or differently.

When contemplating the meaning of The Knight of Swords, ask yourself:

Am I ready to take control of my life?

Am I listening to others for good counsel?

Is my will blinding me to other possibilities?

Are my goals valid and worth the effort?

UPRIGHT

Charging ahead • Overbearing • Determination • Stubbornness

REVERSE

Perversion • Backward • Weakness • Unreliable

Meaning in a Reading

UPRIGHT	REVERSE

Core Meaning

You are hell-bent on getting your mission accomplished. You set out to obtain a goal, and you will stop at nothing to see it to the end. Be sure you are aiming toward progress and not just running wildly away from a problem. Don't let your strong will cloud your better judgment.

Core Meaning

Distractions and chaos have you at full-tilt. You have a deep desire to cut through the noise of life, but can't seem to achieve clarity. Sources you normally count on are unreliable and unstable. You want to make progress, but every time you move ahead it feels like you take several steps backward.

Quick-Read Meanings

LOVE

You want to charge ahead in a new relationship, but that is ill-advised. You might be crazy about that special someone, but pull back.

MONEY

Your financial climate is unstable. Your instinct tells you to cut through the fog and forge ahead. Follow your gut, but be mindful of warning signs and adjust appropriately.

CAREER

There is no denying your enthusiasm about corporate goals. However, others may not share your fervor. Avoid bullying or bossiness.

FAMILY

You are the leader of the family, and you feel you should take charge. Move ahead with your ideas, but not at the expense of ignoring the needs and feelings of family members.

Quick-Read Meanings

LOVE

Something has gone awry in your relationship. It feels like you've lost ground in communicating with your mate. Don't force the issue.

MONEY

It's time for a do-over. You're forced to start over in your financial endeavors. This may feel backward to you, but eventually you will see forward momentum in money matters.

CAREER

You or a colleague is perceived as a weak link within your industry. You have a choice to move through it, or take a different tack.

FAMILY

Wild and unstable behavior from family has you feeling uneasy. Put your foot down. These issues can be controlled, but you must be strong.

THE KNIGHT OF SWORDS SAYS...

"You want to take full charge of your life and stoke the fires of your dreams. The trouble is, other people in your life aren't sure this is the best path for you. Your zest is admirable, but take a hard look at reality, too. Battles are won with a combination of passion and a clear mission. Make sure you have both on your side before charging ahead."

KNIGHT OF SWORDS

QUEEN OF SWORDS.

QUEEN OF SWORDS

This card suggests you are comfortable with the choices you make. You are at ease in your own skin, and happy with what life brings your way. Nonetheless, you are beckoning for more in your life. You feel you can be a better influence, or contribute more to others. You have dreams and ideas you want to send out to the world.

When contemplating the meaning of The Queen of Swords, ask yourself:

Am I getting my needs met?

How can I provide strong comfort to my family?

Why am I distancing myself from others?

Should I soften my attitude?

How can I balance my intellect with compassion?

UPRIGHT

Need • Comfort • Confidence • Assurance

REVERSE

Cruelty • Distant • Icy • Ambitious

Meaning in a Reading

UPRIGHT	REVERSE

Core Meaning

You have needs. Most of them are met, but there is one major requirement you are still seeking to satisfy. You have no fear of the future or the unknown. You are confident and have assurance that your vision will come to fruition. You are in a position of strong leadership, and this does not bother you in the least.

Core Meaning

You are smart, ambitious, and driven. These outstanding qualities are helpful in getting what you want. However, you can be dominating and cold. Your actions and honesty can be brutal toward others. You're sometimes assertive to the point of being cruel. These behaviors stem from feeling unworthy or unaccepted by others.

Quick-Read Meanings

LOVE

Take the high road. This really isn't new advice to you. You know the only way to deal with your partner is with clarity, intelligence, and integrity.

MONEY

You established a comfortable nest egg. Sit on it, and be glad you have it. Avoid the temptation to tamper or fiddle with the funds to come.

CAREER

You have the power to make great improvement. Why aren't you doing it? Embrace your influence and status. Take advantage of your sway.

FAMILY

Whether it's you or another mother figure, the matriarch is expecting you to take more responsibility. Step into a strong mothering role.

Quick-Read Meanings

LOVE

You are distant in the relationship. You are brooding over something, and it's causing you to withdraw yourself from your mate.

MONEY

You have a distinct idea about your finances. The trouble is, they aren't living up to your expectations. Don't force things, but keep your mental ideas about money intact.

CAREER

You may feel justified in your actions, but your assertion is borderline aggressive. Being the boss doesn't have to equate to being bossy and overbearing.

FAMILY

Rifts and separations in the family are likely. You resent shouldering all the responsibility. The more cold you become, the more distant your family will be with you.

QUEEN OF SWORDS

THE QUEEN OF SWORDS SAYS...

"Being in a position of authority has its advantages. You have the chance to make a powerful impact on your family and/or community. Don't be blinded by your own power. Soften your edges a little. You are worthy of respect; you don't have to demand it."

KING OF **SWORDS.**

KING OF SWORDS

You enjoy a position of authority and high status. You are clear about your goals and needs. You feel you have the strength and intelligence to obtain what you want. You get things done with your self-confidence and determination. You employ strategy and cunning to get results.

When contemplating the meaning of The King of Swords, ask yourself:

How can I take healthy advantage of my power?

How can I improve my communication skills?

How can I maintain professionalism and keep my integrity?

Am I making the most of my position in life?

UPRIGHT

Strength • Intellect • Discrimination • Professionalism

REVERSE

Fickle • Unkind • Indecisive • Unfavorable

Meaning in a Reading

UPRIGHT	REVERSE

Core Meaning

You have won acclaim and status. Your professionalism and qualifications are admirable. You have discriminating taste, and you maintain a cool demeanor. You are calm, collected, and in control of your life. You are able to discern what is best for you and your community. You make the right choices.

Core Meaning

You've allowed a distasteful event to overshadow your identity. You have become weak because you let circumstances control you. You lack the strength to carry out responsibility. Your disfavor with others makes you ornery and unpleasant. You don't trust yourself, and waver when making decisions.

Quick-Read Meanings

LOVE

You are absolutely sure about the relationship. You have no doubt about being perfectly paired with your mate. Together you will accomplish great things.

MONEY

Your finances are stable due to shrewd investments. You take responsibility for your money. You spend smartly, and expect others to do the same.

CAREER

You are stable and secure in your work. You anticipate your next move. Take a closer look at legal issues in your career.

FAMILY

A paternal role is established within the family. Security and provision are top priorities. Responsibilities are defined and met.

Quick-Read Meanings

LOVE

Disappointment with your mate gives you a foul attitude. You're thinking about calling off the relationship, but you are unsure.

MONEY

You ignored solid financial advice and now regret it. You aren't being responsible with money. You think money and things will ease your pain, but they won't.

CAREER

You find yourself in new territory at work. This makes you feel insecure and unable to present a strong front among your colleagues.

FAMILY

You feel stuck and caught between conflicting opinions in the family. You want to put your head in the sand and forget everything.

KING OF SWORDS

THE KING OF SWORDS SAYS...

"After a lot of hard work and mental effort, you have finally reached a point of security. You are able to provide for others, and enjoy being generous with your resources. Don't let disappointment or disapproval make you insecure. Being fair and just is your touchstone."

THE SUIT OF CUPS

ACE OF CUPS

You have been given a chance to start over. This new beginning offers great promise. You are feeling hopeful about news you've received, and you can expect great things in your future. You experience great relief because an emotional issue has been resolved. Rely on your intuition and spiritual guidance for continued revelation.

When contemplating the meaning of The Ace of Cups, ask yourself:

Am I ready for a new and promising phase of life?

Am I open to spiritual renewal?

Do my emotions need to be cleansed and purified?

Am I ready for a healing?

UPRIGHT

Fresh start • Healing • Gifts • Spirituality

REVERSE

Endings • Separation • Drained • Waste

Meaning in a Reading

UPRIGHT	REVERSE

Core Meaning

Get ready to receive new spiritual insight that will clear your conscience. You may also experience a physical healing. Wonderful coincidences take place out of the blue. You are gaining stability and employing more moderation in your life.

Core Meaning

There is significant waste taking place in your life. Thoughtlessly giving away precious resources leaves you feeling drained. It is as though you are bleeding, and unable to stop the loss of vital energy.

Quick-Read Meanings

LOVE

You are open to a new love relationship. You feel blessed, as if your cup is overfull with joy.

MONEY

Exerting moderation will help you adjust the flow of your finances. You can expect funding from an unlikely but reliable source.

CAREER

A refreshing shift is happening in your work, and you will thrive.

FAMILY

You take great pleasure from your family. They appreciate how well you care for them, and show their gratitude in sweet, tender ways.

Quick-Read Meanings

LOVE

You have exhausted all your energy on saving a relationship. It's time to consider ending it.

MONEY

It's time to stop wasting your money. Mindless squandering will lead to depletion.

CAREER

You are experiencing an ending in your vocation. Don't let this ending close your attention to other options.

FAMILY

You give, give, and give but it never feels like enough. What's worse is that the family isn't giving back. You can't keep this up. Work to find balance.

THE ACE OF CUPS SAYS...

"Your cup is definitely half full. Optimism is at an all time high because hope and healing are at hand. You are inspired to help others, and receive life-affirming gifts from the universe. Your cup runneth over. Enjoy this delightful time of peace and beauty in your life."

ACE OF CUPS

TWO OF CUPS

You are forming a new partnership that shows much promise. This could be a personal or professional alliance. Communications bring about new understanding. Equal share of duties and resources make the household harmonious. Innovations in medicine are helpful and interesting to you.

When contemplating the meaning of The Two of Cups, ask yourself:

How can I promote healing in my life?

How can I help and heal others?

How can I communicate better in my relationships?

How can I employ more balance to benefit my partnerships?

UPRIGHT

Health • Partnership • Understanding • Cooperation

REVERSE

Incompatible • Poor choices • Refusal • Separation

Meaning in a Reading

UPRIGHT	REVERSE

Core Meaning

You are more clear about your ideas of a healthy relationship. You know that give and take are essential for forming successful alliances. New insights about healing are revolutionary. You're considering alternative, holistic medicine.

Core Meaning

You are making poor choices that don't honor who you are. A sense of unworthiness makes you refuse goodness in your life. You want health and wellness, but you don't want to let others into your heart.

Quick-Read Meanings

LOVE

Engagement, marriage, or a firm commitment to your relationship is taking place. You are sure about your partnership with your soul mate.

Quick-Read Meanings

LOVE

You are going through a separation. This ending is due to mutual incompatibility. Don't let bitterness poison your love life in the future.

MONEY

You gain ground on your finances due to a helpful partnership.

MONEY

You are being stingy with your resources. You are cutting off your funding and refusing to share.

CAREER

The health industry is attractive to you right now. You feel the need to help others feel better and excel in life.

CAREER

You may feel obligated to keep working in an unfitting environment, but eventually you will have to move to a more compatible venue.

FAMILY

Family is your main source of pride. You and your partner are able to see your family succeed. Your home is happy and prosperous.

FAMILY

Separation and disharmony in the home is caused by refusal to communicate. Someone in the family is dealing with imbalances in health. Try talking about it and actively listening to concerns.

THE TWO OF CUPS SAYS...

"Your relationships are thriving, and you finally feel understood. You have clarity of purpose, and you know the only way to succeed is by accepting help from others. The healing arts are particularly interesting to you at this time. Home and family are a source of pride and a top priority."

THREE OF CUPS

Raise your glass and toast to your good health. This is a time of celebration and giving thanks for bounty, abundance, and good fortune. You appreciate the finer things in life. Beauty is all around you, and you relish sharing it with others. New friendships blossom and warm your heart. Social gatherings bring joy and inspiration.

When contemplating the meaning of The Three of Cups, ask yourself:

Is it time to be more sociable?

Am I ready to celebrate my accomplishments?

Am I taking time to appreciate the finer things in life?

How can I have a good time without overdoing it?

Can I relax and just enjoy the moment?

UPRIGHT

Charm • Joy • Jubilation • Creativity

REVERSE

Overindulgence • Irrational • Obsession • Bad influence

Meaning in a Reading

UPRIGHT	REVERSE

Core Meaning

New friends, partnerships, and family additions are cause for celebration. You are a social butterfly, and networking reaps positive benefits. People are drawn to you, and you bring joy to others. A surge of creativity spikes your energy levels and keeps you inspired.

Core Meaning

Overindulging and partying are affecting you in negative ways. You are losing friends and shirking responsibilities. You are not being rational about your choices. You are keeping company with a bad crowd. You may think the party life is fun, but it's really an attempt to fill a void and it's stealing your joy.

Quick-Read Meanings

LOVE

A honeymoon getaway or exotic vacation with your partner is in order. Get away from the rat race and enjoy an invigorating escape together.

MONEY

You may not have won the lottery, but you can finally enjoy the financial fruits of your labor.

CAREER

You're thinking about, or have already launched into, an entrepreneurial endeavor with friends. You have plenty to celebrate. Your plans are promising.

FAMILY

Christenings, graduations, and/or marriages are likely. Merriment and joy bless your home. You welcome a new addition to the family.

Quick-Read Meanings

LOVE

You are making harsh, irrational judgments against your partner because you feel undeserving of his/her love.

MONEY

People are taking advantage of you. Not everybody you give to is worthy of your charitable kindness.

CAREER

Gossip around the water cooler has cast you in a bad light. Take pride in yourself and your work. Remember that gossip is born from envy.

FAMILY

Check out suspicious behavior exhibited by family members. Your loved ones might be indulging in bad behavior due to negative influences. Irrational choices are made to gain acceptance from the group.

THE THREE OF CUPS SAYS...

"Live, laugh, love. Moments of sharing with friends and family are long-lasting treasures. You have the chance to make beautiful memories. You reap the rewards of hard work. You have adequate support and backing for your ideas. Love is at the heart of your relationships."

FOUR OF CUPS

You have several options in front of you, and only one is the right choice to make. You know this, but you are blocked by fear, inaction, or doubt. You have grown in your faith and your heart is willing, but challenges leave you with depleted energy. Stubbornness and willfulness keep you from doing the right thing. You have a bright idea, but you don't have the confidence or experience to implement it.

When contemplating the meaning of The Four of Cups, ask yourself:

Am I missing out on a great opportunity?

Is there an important detail I'm overlooking?

How can I work better in a team setting?

How can I develop my confidence?

Why am I hesitating?

UPRIGHT

Doubt • Insecurity • Inspiration • Hesitation

REVERSE

Disappointment • Rejection • Inexperience • Depression

Meaning in a Reading

UPRIGHT	REVERSE

Core Meaning

Inspiration has struck, but you are too unsure about yourself to take action. Insecurity makes you hesitant to proceed. Don't let self-doubt overtake your forward mobility. You have the wisdom and support to act on your ideas.

Core Meaning

You see others enjoy love and pleasure, but you feel separated from that side of life. Depression keeps you from experiencing joy. You fear rejection, and life feels like a disappointment. Lack of experience intimidates you and keeps you from trying new things.

Quick-Read Meanings

LOVE

You are being approached, but you're not sure if this kind of love is right for you. Someone is reaching out, but you have reservations.

MONEY

A grand opportunity is being handed to you, but for some reason you aren't accepting. Be clear about your choice to decline a sweet financial deal.

CAREER

You recognize teamwork as an essential element in getting your job done, but you don't want to participate. Question your motives for denying teamwork.

FAMILY

You have been working with a troubled member of your family. Autism or struggling with communication is an issue. Work to find a common link that will shatter communication barriers.

Quick-Read Meanings

LOVE

You don't feel deserving of love. This is partly due to failed relationships you blame yourself for in the past. Work to heal your emotions, and grow more mature about love matters.

MONEY

You don't have enough experience to manage your money. Don't let lack of credit defeat you. Start building your money-sense one step at a time.

CAREER

A missed promotion or advancement is a great disappointment. Don't take rejection at work personally. You were overlooked because you need more experience in your field.

FAMILY

You are disappointed with yourself, and feel you could do more to be valuable to the family. Realize you are loved for who you are—not what you do.

THE FOUR OF CUPS SAYS...

"Don't let a hit to your self-confidence spoil the pleasures life has to offer. Open your heart. Realize you are valuable and special. An excellent opportunity is right in front of you, but you're letting insecurity and unworthiness get in the way of growth. You have the support you need to grow."

FIVE OF CUPS

You have lost in love, and it has caused emotional trauma. You are at a crossroads, and are unsure about how to proceed. Sometimes it feels as though you cannot go on. You may feel isolated—like an outcast—or that no one understands you. You must recognize that not all hope is lost. There are people in your life who love you and believe in you. You can turn things around, you just need to look up and recognize potential.

When contemplating the meaning of The Five of Cups, ask yourself:

Am I letting past failures keep me from future success?

Is it time to move beyond betrayal?

How is loss keeping me from growing and moving forward?

How can I be more constructive and make life better?

UPRIGHT

Rejection • Depression • Neglect • Failure

REVERSE

Contemplation • Solidarity • Resourcefulness • Strong-willed

Meaning in a Reading

UPRIGHT	REVERSE

Core Meaning

You are kicking yourself for a failure. You may be partly responsible, but taking all the blame is self-defeating. You have a chance to take a better path in life. You just need to clarify what you want, and start moving in a better direction.

Core Meaning

Innovation and creativity are big themes in your life. You have solidified your ideas and are ready to put your resources to work in a positive direction. The problem is, you are going to have to make your dreams come true by yourself.

Quick-Read Meanings

LOVE

Don't let failures or poor choices in love ruin you for a great relationship in the future.

MONEY

Your finances are going to get better, but you need to think positive. Take advantage of resources that are still viable. Don't dwell on past failures.

CAREER

Staying stuck in the same function and routine is depressing. Carve a better career out for yourself.

FAMILY

A member of your family cannot be reached. You have tried to communicate, but your attempts have failed. Don't let this loss cause you to neglect other family members who need you.

Quick-Read Meanings

LOVE

Investing in a relationship takes a back seat. You are focused on bettering yourself before starting a partnership.

MONEY

You are standing on solid financial ground while everyone around you is struggling. Don't let the failure of others tip you over.

CAREER

You want to invest your skills in a new direction, but it seems overwhelming to do so. Rely on your beliefs.

FAMILY

The house is a mess, the family is chaotic, and it seems you are the only one who cares. You may have to establish order in the home all by yourself.

THE FIVE OF CUPS SAYS...

"Everybody experiences failure and setbacks. You are not alone in dealing with mistakes. You don't have to walk through life alone, but the only one who can deal with your burdens is you. Don't become overwhelmed with negativity. Look around you. There is so much life has to offer. You are supported in ways you can't see."

FIVE OF CUPS

SIX OF CUPS

You want to recapture better times of the past. Nostalgia consumes you, and you desire to return to the "good old days." A need for simplicity and country life may be calling to you. New love relationships and friendships are on the horizon. You seek the beauty in simple pleasures. Children and causes that support child development are very important. You're considering volunteer work or contributing to a non-profit organization. You are a sweet influence in your community.

When contemplating the meaning of The Six of Cups, ask yourself:

How can I beautify my world more?

How can I positively contribute to my community?

How can I allow the good times in the past to color my future?

How can I give more value to the children in my life?

UPRIGHT

Nostalgia • Simplicity • Giving • Innocence

REVERSE

Scarcity • Stingy • Bitter • Retrospection

Meaning in a Reading

UPRIGHT	REVERSE

Core Meaning

You find yourself reminiscing and feeling wistful about the past. You want to simplify your life. Service to others and volunteer work is a keen interest. Beautifying your environment is a priority. Children bring joy and innocence to your life.

Core Meaning

Lack of abundance has you feeling pinched and bitter. You are stingy with your resources. You have forgotten that giving a little kindness to others can go a long way to brightening your world. You are living in the past, and refuse to move forward.

Quick-Read Meanings

LOVE

Thinking about a past love brings sweet memories. You desire to recapture youthful romance.

MONEY

Fundraising and charity become prime interests for you. Consider donating money to worthy non-profit organizations in the community.

CAREER

Career is focused on giving back and helping people. Your work is a positive influence with far-reaching effects.

FAMILY

Memories of family members in the past have you longing for how things were. Appreciating the good times gives you a chance to employ more beauty and simplicity in the family today. Children are a source of delight, and remind you to play more.

Quick-Read Meanings

LOVE

Your expectations are too high. You want more, but your partner is unable to give.

MONEY

Your finances are meager, and you are looking at old-fashioned ways to save money. Sewing, gardening, and reusing old materials are helpful.

CAREER

You remember when you first started your career and wish it could be that way again. Continuing to live in the past threatens to make you bitter and stuck.

FAMILY

The whole family gathers to pitch in. Everyone must work to contribute to the needs of the household. Strict understanding about the differences between "wants" and "needs" must be defined.

THE SIX OF CUPS SAYS...

"It's been said, 'you can never go home again.' In a sense, this is true—but you can take the treasures of the past and savor them in the present. Sharing memories with friends and family can recapture better days. Taking an active, positive role in the community is a way to honor old-fashioned values. Relishing the company of children is a reminder of youthful joy. Giving and sharing beauty with the world opens your heart so beauty can flow back to you."

SEVEN OF CUPS

The Seven of Cups represents limitless possibilities and potential. You are surrounded by opportunity, you just have to reach out and grab it. You are the master of your destiny, and you have the power to make the right choices for your best interest. You have many projects in the air right now. You have a lot on your mind, and sometimes it is hard to focus.

When contemplating the meaning of The Seven of Cups, ask yourself:

How can I channel my focus and make the right choice?

Can I manage my thoughts and tasks better?

Can I see the opportunities right before my eyes?

Am I open to new possibilities?

Do I have all the details?

UPRIGHT

Opportunity • Possibility • Potential • Multitasking

REVERSE

Chaos • Indecision • Overwhelmed • Undeserving

Meaning in a Reading

UPRIGHT	REVERSE

Core Meaning

You are having to manage a lot of affairs, and multitasking is essential. Thoughts of the past influence your future decisions. You have many options in front of you. Get all the details to make an educated decision.

Core Meaning

There may be plenty of opportunity, but you're not seeing it. Feeling insecure or undeserving makes you powerless to make choices. You are overwhelmed with too many distractions. Confusion and chaos threaten to take control.

Quick-Read Meanings

LOVE

No relationship is perfect. Accepting the good with the bad in your partnership opens up new understanding. Love offers many levels of growth.

MONEY

Money matters are looking up. Numerous opportunities for enhancing your finances are at your fingertips.

CAREER

There are several directions you can go if you're looking for a career move. Diversifying is essential. Consider getting more education in a field of interest.

FAMILY

Family life is hectic, and there is a lot of activity in the home. Be selective about what demands your attention or you may become drained.

Quick-Read Meanings

LOVE

Proposing too many options is overwhelming. Your partner may be pulling away due to feeling intimidated by the diversity you are presenting. Keep it simple.

MONEY

Your finances are too spread out. You're having a hard time controlling money flow. You feel drained from trying to keep track of everything.

CAREER

You're tempted to turn your back on work or a project. Too many setbacks and conflicting opinions make you doubt what step to take next.

FAMILY

Your attention is pulled in so many directions you are neglecting someone who really needs you. Quiet the chaos at home and focus on love.

SEVEN OF CUPS

THE SEVEN OF CUPS SAYS...

"Close your eyes and envision all the resources you need. You have the power to summon amazing gifts and opportunities. You have the chance to hone your multi-tasking and management skills. Don't become overwhelmed by your thoughts, or too distracted by the bustle of the world."

EIGHT OF CUPS

Your intuition is guiding you in new directions. You are supported in travel and relocations. You completed a goal or achieved a dream, and now you're ready to move on to the next project. You have the knowledge and resources to make a better life for yourself. You have the strength to take on new challenges.

When contemplating the meaning of The Eight of Cups, ask yourself:

How can I move to higher ground in my relationships?

Is the timing right to make a transition?

Am I running away? Why?

Where am I most needed?

Am I ready for new challenges?

UPRIGHT

Transition • Timing • Progress • Travel

REVERSE

Fleeing • Trouble • Confusion • Rejection

Meaning in a Reading

UPRIGHT	REVERSE

Core Meaning

You worked hard to establish good relationships, and now you are expanding your social network. You are seeking new resources to enhance your love, work, and life. Travel is inspiring and gives you new ideas. You feel like this is a perfect time to start a new phase in life.

Core Meaning

You are saying goodbye to something or someone you love. You may feel like running away is the only option to make things right. Be sure you're not leaving because you are confused or feeling guilty. Running away from trouble will only result in more problems.

Quick-Read Meanings

LOVE

Turn away from past hang-ups and emotional wounds in order to move on. Purify your emotions so you can experience stability in love.

MONEY

You are searching for just the right venture or investment. Make sure you maintain the finances you already established before starting something new.

CAREER

You've been waiting for the right timing to launch into a new career path. This time is now. You have the proper backing, education, and skills to succeed.

FAMILY

Business trips or travel take you away from family. You have a loving, stable foundation. The family supports what you need to do, even if it means being away from home for awhile.

Quick-Read Meanings

LOVE

Thoughts of separation should be addressed. You've established security but the relationship is going through a rocky time. Be clear whether you can salvage what you have before walking away.

MONEY

Finances are topsy-turvy. Ignoring money troubles compounds the difficulties. Use resources at hand to gain higher ground.

CAREER

You've built a strong foundation and reputation at your work. Challenges cropping up tempt you to throw away all the good work you've done.

FAMILY

When the going gets tough, the thing to do is tough it out. Resist the urge to reject members who make your life complicated.

THE EIGHT OF CUPS SAYS...

"Difficulties are nothing new to you. You have emotional clarity about the next step to take. This move might be a big one and saying goodbye may be bittersweet. Your travels will uplift you and put you in a better position. Trust your intuition about timing to reach your goals. Take advantage of resources at hand to help you make progress."

NINE OF CUPS

You are sitting pretty! This card is often referred to as the "wish card." Dreams and goals have been realized. You are satisfied with your relationships. Health and wealth are stabilized. You enjoy a sense of security and contentment.

When contemplating the meaning of The Nine of Cups, ask yourself:

Am I grateful for the blessings in my life?

Am I willing to share myself and my resources?

How can I maintain contentment and satisfaction?

Am I protecting my assets?

Do I recognize the support available to me?

UPRIGHT

Satisfaction • Contentment • Accomplishment • Winning

REVERSE

Greedy • Defensive • Reluctant • Restrictive

Meaning in a Reading

UPRIGHT	REVERSE

Core Meaning

Your social network is healthy and expansive. Friends and family are supportive. You have worked hard to achieve goals, and now you can enjoy the rewards. You feel like a winner in love, health, and wealth. You feel accomplished, and you're in a great place in life.

Core Meaning

You are being stingy with your resources. Perhaps a time of starvation physically or emotionally has compelled you to hoard and keep everything to yourself. You restrict your generosity, and get defensive when others want things from you. You feel tight and constricted.

Quick-Read Meanings

LOVE

You have confidence in love. You know you are emotionally mature enough to start and maintain healthy relationships.

MONEY

Finances are substantial enough to spend on extra luxuries. You may be enjoying a monetary gift or inheritance.

CAREER

You worked hard to bolster your confidence, education, and skills. Your efforts allow you to win success and enjoy prestige at work.

FAMILY

Children may be grown and you are enjoying their success in life. You reap the rewards of investing in the family, and enjoy seeing them thrive.

Quick-Read Meanings

LOVE

Being selfish in the relationship is taking a toll. You are possessive and controlling with your partner.

MONEY

You are inflexible with money. Overprotection of resources and greed are stifling the opportunity for financial growth.

CAREER

You are unwilling to accept support from your peers at work. You are defensive about your ideas. Sharing your plans makes you feel vulnerable and exposed.

FAMILY

You have a specific idea how the family should be run. When your expectations aren't met, you get stern and bullish. Your way might not be the best way.

THE NINE OF CUPS SAYS...

"Having a winning attitude is half the trick to winning in life. The other half is maintaining your emotional and physical health. You are in a prime position to succeed in all areas of life. You have a beautiful network of loved ones who support and admire you. You exude confidence and charisma. Be mindful to share yourself and your resources. Don't staunch the flow of good luck by constricting your generosity."

TEN OF CUPS

You are living the dream! Healthy relationships with friends and family—especially children—are a source of wonder and joy. Creativity is precious to you, and you have interest in artful pursuits. You place high value on your health, and are taking better care of yourself. You are inspired to move in positive directions, and you feel supported.

When contemplating the meaning of The Ten of Cups, ask yourself:

Am I ready to embrace my highest potential?

Am I grateful for my family?

Do I feel a sense of hope and promise?

How can I maintain harmony and emotional balance?

How can I express gratitude for the gifts I've received?

UPRIGHT

Idyllic • Promise • Abundance • Flourishing

REVERSE

Incompletion • Pleading • Separation • Drained

Meaning in a Reading

UPRIGHT	REVERSE

Core Meaning

You can breathe easy. Barricades in the past are just a memory. You have a clear understanding of the meaning of true value. Areas of health, emotion, and family experience a renewal. You feel as though limitless potential is yours to tap into. Spread your wings and fly!

Core Meaning

Spinning your wheels and expending your energy excessively has left you feeling drained. Separations from loved ones may be an issue. You feel incomplete and unfulfilled. You are pleading for help, but it feels like your requests fall on deaf ears.

Quick-Read Meanings

LOVE

A beautiful blossom is unfolding in your love life. You released past grudges and can give your heart freely now.

MONEY

The promise of financial gain has become a reality. Your finances flourish. You consider real estate for investment potential.

CAREER

You followed a rainbow of dreams, and now you have access to the pot of gold. Others may have thought you were wishfully thinking, but are now amazed how your wishes are coming true in your career.

FAMILY

You enjoy harmony and easy times in the family. Children are happy, and another bundle of joy may be on the way. Plans to obtain a new, better home for the family are promising.

Quick-Read Meanings

LOVE

Major disagreements about children or money is posing a rift in the relationship. You feel drained, and are considering a separation.

MONEY

Your finances are drained. This is partly due to over-indulgence and wasteful spending.

CAREER

You question a career move, and have doubts if this new direction is right for you. You feel incomplete and are looking for professional satisfaction.

FAMILY

Emotions raise to a boil, and running away is tempting. Children are a source of conflict. Custody might be an issue.

TEN OF CUPS

THE TEN OF CUPS SAYS...

"Somewhere over the rainbow you have found your pot of gold. Dreams of financial, familial, and true love fulfillment are within your grasp. Reap the beautiful bounty shimmering in your life. Keep your heart open and enjoy emotional clarity. Incorporate more play and creativity in your life to sustain joy."

PAGE OF CUPS

You are playing the part of the dandy, and loving it. You have a pure understanding of your emotions, and trust your feelings. Your social scene is vibrant and full of promise. You are a highly valued friend. People seek you out for advice and intuitive guidance. Interest in creative expression is keen, particularly in fashion.

When contemplating the meaning of The Page of Cups, ask yourself:

How can I enjoy my freedom?

Am I following my intuition?

How can I implement more creativity in my work?

How can I maintain loving and generosity in my relationships?

How can I embrace my differences?

UPRIGHT

Sophistication • Culture • Confidence • Insightful

REVERSE

Unaccepted • Disillusioned • Disappointment • Apathy

Meaning in a Reading

UPRIGHT	REVERSE

Core Meaning

You have a unique outlook on life, and people love that about you. You are sophisticated and always seeking ways to better yourself. You have an interest in culture, and consider travel as a way to learn more. You are highly intuitive, and use your insights to help others. Creativity in spiritual sciences and art is blossoming in loving, beautiful ways.

Core Meaning

You can't understand the world, or why people treat you so poorly. You are different, and even though you feel this is an asset, others don't agree. People disappoint you because they can't see beauty in uniqueness. Your disillusionment with the world has made you apathetic. You allow circumstances to tarnish your shine and dim your light.

Quick-Read Meanings

LOVE

You are loving and giving. You enjoy passion and sensuality. You know there are plenty of fish in the sea, and exploration in the oceans of love is exciting.

MONEY

Making money is easy. You know how to tap resources, and you employ unique strategies to gain income.

CAREER

Your business in a creative industry flourishes. Art, music, and social settings are ideal work outlets. Even if you find your current career uninspiring, you can introduce more creativity in your work.

FAMILY

You feel like your family could use a fresh, new look. Give your home a facelift, and introduce more freedom and joy in the family.

Quick-Read Meanings

LOVE

You're looking for love in all the wrong places. Disappointments make you want to give up on love.

MONEY

You are disappointed because money plans have gone awry. You don't understand why this happened, and your disillusionment is prohibiting progress.

CAREER

You think your plans and ideas at work are fantastic, but others don't share your views. This gets you down and gives you a poor attitude at work.

FAMILY

You or a member of the family are rebelling. There is a specific idea about how the family should look, but someone isn't conforming to that image.

PAGE OF CUPS

 ## THE PAGE OF CUPS SAYS...

"Being different is a good thing. Celebrate your own style and share it with the world. Follow your insights and help others with your intuitive wisdom. Creativity brings renewal and fresh perspectives. Emotional purification makes you feel strong and capable of taking on the world."

KNIGHT OF CUPS

KNIGHT OF CUPS.

You have substance, skill, and savvy. This puts you in a position to implement your ideas and forge your dreams into reality. You are inspired to take charge of your life. You have noble integrity and clear ideas about right and wrong. You live by high standards and feel others should, too. Perfectionism and intense attention to detail is both hindering and helpful sometimes.

When contemplating the meaning of The Knight of Cups, ask yourself:

Am I prepared for a new, exciting quest?

How can I show more honor and respect?

Is my integrity helping or hindering?

Are my high standards reasonable and healthy?

Am I ready to put my dreams and thoughts into action?

UPRIGHT

Expectations • Chivalry • Superiority • Idealism

REVERSE

Boastful • Strain • Dominating • Force

Meaning in a Reading

UPRIGHT	REVERSE

Core Meaning

You feel compelled to improve the world, and your chivalrous pursuits are admirable. You have high expectations of others which can bring out the best in them. However, sometimes your overconfidence can make people feel inferior. You see no reason why the world shouldn't run as you see fit.

Core Meaning

Egotism is a major demon you struggle with. Overconfidence and boastfulness prohibit you from maintaining healthy relationships personally and professionally. Forcing your will can be abusive at times. You want love, but you push it away with your bullish demeanor.

Quick-Read Meanings

LOVE

You or your mate is a knight in shining armor. Respect and honor are valued in the relationship. Working together to meet goals is key.

MONEY

You are focused and capable of seeing your financial ideals to fruition. You may have to cross into unknown territory, but once you do the money will flow.

CAREER

You have a vision for your business, and will stop at nothing to see it to reality. You have high standards, and expect others to follow your lead.

FAMILY

Family looks to you as a shining example. You run a tight ship at home, and sometimes this is taxing to family members. In the long-run, however, your enforcement of high standards will pay off.

Quick-Read Meanings

LOVE

You are totally lovable. You don't have to shove your worth down your partner's throat to get him/her to love you. Forceful or controlling behaviors push a loved one away.

MONEY

You got cocky with your investments, and you're feeling the sting of consequences. You can salvage a monetary loss, but you will have to humble yourself.

CAREER

You blew up at the office because others didn't comply to your demands. Rather than blame others for failure, look to yourself for answers.

FAMILY

A strained relationship with a family member makes you redouble your position. Inflexible certainty that you are right is making family members feel wrong. This brews feelings of resentment.

 THE KNIGHT OF CUPS SAYS...

"Your armor is gleaming because you have polished it to perfection. This armor symbolizes your skill, wisdom, and vision. You have every reason and resource to charge ahead with your dreams. Moving into the unknown does not intimidate you. Your innate sense of right and wrong is as accurate as a compass."

QUEEN OF CUPS

Life has handed you vital, sometimes hard lessons. Rather than letting hardships get you down, you converted these challenges into positive growing pains. Your experience has given you clarity about what is important. You protect value with grace and poise. You have amazing intellectual focus and your psychic perception is keen.

When contemplating the meaning of The Queen of Cups, ask yourself:

Am I clear about authentic value?

Am I protecting my assets well enough?

Am I a good mentor and example?

Do I trust my instincts and follow my intuition?

Do I value my dreams and pay attention to them?

UPRIGHT

Protection • Intuition • Concentration • Poise

REVERSE

Unfaithful • Unhappy • Dishonest • Grudges

Meaning in a Reading

UPRIGHT	REVERSE

Core Meaning

Life has made you prioritize, and protecting your interests is key. Family and children are precious; you have a vested interest in their growth. You are in control of resources, and you take this responsibility seriously. Through concentrated intuition you are able to make things happen. People see you as a leader. You recognize this, and accept the role with grace and humility.

Core Meaning

You are lying to yourself and refuse to listen to your inner voice. Emotional and/or substance abuse clouds your judgment. You are unhappy with how your life has turned out and resent others who are happy. You hold grudges from past hurts. Self-sabotage is a major theme. You do things to thwart your joy and success.

Quick-Read Meanings

LOVE

You sense emotions in your partner stirring under the surface. Follow your instincts, and open a dialogue about what is troubling him/her.

MONEY

You have a hunch that if you wait in confident expectation, your financial gain will unfold on its own. Follow your gut.

CAREER

As a leader, you are expected to delegate and dole out vital resources to the team. You take pride in your responsibilities, and people admire your integrity.

FAMILY

Your mothering side is in full force. Nurturing and supporting your family is a priority. Trust your intuition to help family stay on track.

Quick-Read Meanings

LOVE

Infidelity damages your relationships. You are looking to people and things to fill a void. Seek guidance or counseling to recognize your self-worth.

MONEY

You made a promise but you're backing out. Dishonesty and shady tactics are used to make money.

CAREER

A cold, uncaring attitude is choking all the joy from your job. You've forgotten the value of accomplishment and integrity.

FAMILY

You've given up on trying to get a handle on the chaos at home. Poor judgment and dishonesty are hot-button issues.

QUEEN OF CUPS

THE QUEEN OF CUPS SAYS...

"You are the queen of your realm, and you earned every inch of respect. Thankfully, you don't abuse your position of power. Rather, you earnestly accept your role with an open heart. You skillfully manage resources, and delegate with diplomacy and tact. Loving kindness is your touchstone, and you treat others with respect. Your confidence and maturity allow you to give yourself to others without losing your identity."

KING OF **CUPS.**

KING OF CUPS

You are emotionally secure enough in yourself to show tenderness without worrying about it being construed as weakness. You have great responsibilities, but you are able to shoulder them with ease. You have gained insights through experience and use this to your advantage. You receive intuitive impressions and follow them without question.

When contemplating the meaning of The King of Cups, ask yourself:

How can I use my status in effective, honorable ways?

Am I a stable, admirable leader?

How can my intuition and perception help me?

How can I ensure power doesn't control me?

How can I be strong without being intimidating?

UPRIGHT

Self-assured • Perceptive • Authority • Strength

REVERSE

Uncaring • Calculating • Unpredictable • Untrustworthy

Meaning in a Reading

UPRIGHT	REVERSE

Core Meaning

If life were a poker game, you would be a high roller. Why? Because you can read others like a book. You know their tells and perceive unspoken messages easily. You also maintain an impressive poker face. You put up a strong front, and rarely crack under pressure. You know what it takes to manage your responsibilities, and take pleasure in your authority.

Core Meaning

The taste of power has made you hungry for more. The need for control may manifest in substance abuse, or abuse of others. You can be calculating and cruel in your pursuit of personal gratification. Others are hesitant to trust you due to unpredictable mood swings.

Quick-Read Meanings

LOVE

Your partner needs you to be strong. Personal problems require you to step up and take care of your mate.

MONEY

You deal with money problems with integrity and strength. Consequently, others see your value, and pay you for your worth.

CAREER

You are at the top of your career, and you feel rock-solid about your future. You may have to travel for work. You take challenges in stride and remain stable.

FAMILY

A strong fatherly figure is worthy of respect. Advice from this paternal influence is sound and just. Honor and healthy discipline is important in the home.

Quick-Read Meanings

LOVE

You or your partner is being manipulative. Intense desire to get needs met manifests in unhealthy, erratic behavior.

MONEY

You got paid, but feel you deserve more. A sense of entitlement is damaging your integrity and attitude.

CAREER

Your uncaring attitude toward your performance at work makes your superiors question your value. You appear unpredictable and a risk to the company.

FAMILY

Being demanding at home pushes family members away. You say and do things without consideration to others' feelings. Family sees you as unstable and unworthy of trust.

KING OF CUPS

THE KING OF CUPS SAYS...

"It's good to be king. Ruling your realm isn't easy, but luckily you've gained a lot of experience over time. Intense self-investment leads to self-assurance. People admire you, and you are a trustworthy resource. You perceive subtle details that give you an edge. Your strength is a source of security and comfort to others. You have control over your emotions, and are a worthy ruler."

READING THE CARDS

READING BASICS

HANDLING THE CARDS

The Tarot is a mirror. It reflects back an image of who you are and what your life looks like. Consider making yourself and your mirror as clean and spotless as possible. Doing so will produce the clearest reflection of yourself while looking through the sparkling mirror of the Tarot.

How you handle the cards will depend upon your relationship to the Tarot. Think of the Tarot as an extension of yourself. To perform your best, you know you need to eat right, exercise, and get enough rest. For your partnership with the Tarot to work optimally, it requires similar commitment. Forethought, preparation, and soulful investment are integral to handling the cards and to successful readings.

PREPARATION

Before a hand is laid on your deck, it's a good idea to take a few quiet moments to cleanse your thoughts and hone your intuition. You can do this by closing your eyes, taking a few refreshing deep breaths, and getting attuned to your inner energy.

Because the Tarot is a system of wisdom based on spiritual philosophies, consider saying a prayer or devotional before handling the cards. The more centered, tranquil, and purified you are, the better your results will be with the Tarot.

In addition to meditation and prayer before a reading, some Tarot readers light a devotional candle and burn incense. You may also entertain the idea of putting on some relaxing ambient music to soothe your mind, calm your nerves, and put you in a state of relaxation.

CLEANSING THE CARDS

Some Tarot readers conduct a ceremony called smudging the cards. Smudging is a way of cleansing your deck. The idea is to rid the cards of residual energy from previous uses. White sage is a common smudging tool, but you can use your favorite incense. How often you cleanse your cards is up to you. Most Tarot practitioners elect to purify their decks after each reading.

To cleanse and recharge your cards, light a smudge stick (or incense stick), and let the smoke envelop your deck. As you do this, focus your intention on purification and renewal. Close your eyes, relax, and imagine things that represent renewal to you. You might imagine your cards bathed in a beautiful white light; or visualize crystal clear waters gently flowing through the cards, restoring each card to its pure state. Envision your deck being wiped clean of all residual energy. Visualize the sacred smoke wafting away all impurities from the cards. Be sure to conduct your smudging ceremony in a ventilated area. This gives the residual energy a way to exit the room.

SHUFFLING AND CUTTING

Each reader has their own way of handling and shuffling the cards. Whether you riffle the cards or use an overhand shuffle will depend on your preference. Tarot cards are larger than standard playing cards, so you may find the riffling method (also known as the dovetail shuffle) awkward. There is no right or wrong way to shuffle. Allow your intuition be your guide.

Speaking of intuition, it is important to inject your thoughts and energy into the cards as you handle them. The more you clearly project your intent into the Tarot, the clearer your results will be. Keep your questions and objectives in your forethoughts as you shuffle, cut, and pull the cards.

Before pulling the cards, it is customary to cut the deck. Typically the deck is cut three times, as three is a powerful number of creativity and inspiration. If you are reading for someone else, you may ask your querent to cut the deck so his/her energy and intentions are imbued into the cards.

After you collect the cuts, it's time to dole out the cards. The most practiced method of pulling cards is to first set the deck face down and spread out the cards in a fan formation. Fanning out the cards allows them to be displayed individually for ease of pulling. You can ask your querent to pull the

cards. Having your querent pull the cards initiates energetic contact with the deck. This contact promotes clearer messages about what's going on in your querent's life. On the other hand, you may choose to pull the cards yourself. If you do, simply maintain your focus on your querent while pulling. Keep your intention set on highest good and best guidance. Pull the cards one by one, keeping them face down.

The next few pages will offer suggestions and insights into card positions along with phrasing your questions and answers which will help your reading skills.

CARD POSITIONS

Each card of the Tarot possesses meaning and truth on its own merit. When you bring several cards together in a reading, the meanings begin to create a story about what's going on in your life.

Card positions are key in order to make sense of that narrative. Each position is a question, goal, or object linked to your Tarot inquiries. The card you place on top of each position is the answer, action, or clarification to the intent posed by the position.

For example, let's say you have concerns about selling your house. You can create a card position based on that inquiry. You can also create supporting positions that will encourage further information. In this example, you could assign a card position for the condition of the real estate market, the timing in which the house will be sold, or even a position for what kind of buyers are looking for your home.

Keep your meanings for the card positions as simple as possible. Using the hypothetical house-selling scenario, here is an example of assigning positions to get answers to that inquiry:

My House   When to Sell it   How to Sell it

In this example, you can see how the card positions establish a focus. The positions are the question, the cards you pull and place on top of the positions are the answer.

Keep the intent and meaning of the position in mind as you interpret the card you pulled to put in its place. Consider the card and the position as a dialogue, like a conversation between placement and card.

If you're having difficulty understanding the card's question in relation to the position, you can pull another card for clarification. Lay this additional card on top of the original. This new card does not discount the meaning of the original one; combine the meaning of this card with that of the initial one pulled. Pulling an extra card for clarity offers additional information that helps the original card make sense.

REVERSALS

The card meanings in this book are subject to change according to whether a card is pulled upright or upside down. Upside down cards are called *reversals*.

Reversals express a contradiction of the upright meaning. Drawing a card upside down may suggest a reversal of fortune and progress. Reversed cards in a reading commonly indicate loss or taking a step backward on your path. Reversals may also hint to delays and setbacks depending upon the card meaning. In simplest terms, a reversed card in your reading implies the opposite of the upright meaning.

Basic meanings for reversals are provided in this book for each card. It's important to know that reading reversals in the cards is your option. Many Tarot readers (especially beginners) choose to ignore reversals. The choice is yours. If you find reversals overwhelming and confusing, read the Tarot cards using only the upright meanings at first. Later, as you progress in your understanding of the cards, consider adding reversed meanings for more diverse readings. If you opt to not read reversals, be sure to go through your deck making sure all the cards are upright before a reading. This ensures the cards you pull will all be right side up, thus eliminating the occurrence of reversals altogether.

DROPPED CARDS

Occasionally a card will pop out of the deck while you're shuffling, or one might fall to the floor as you're pulling the cards. Because the Tarot is loaded with sensitive, mysterious power, you might want to pay attention to that "wild" card. Sometimes a renegade card might be just the answer you need to an inquiry posed in a position.

If you choose to acknowledge stray cards, have a predetermined position for them, perhaps to the upper left area of your spread. Also pre-establish a meaning for these random cards, perhaps a position with a meaning of "Fate" or "Outside Influence." Dropped cards in this meaningful position will imply a random event or unexpected source that will influence your fate. A stray card in this position will offer clarification about an unexpected event that relates to the other cards you've positioned in your spread.

HOW TO ASK QUESTIONS WITH THE TAROT

Framing an appropriate, heartfelt question for the Tarot is a vital step in the process of reading the cards for insight. Why? Because formulating the right question forces you to focus thoughts on your life and circumstances.

The nature of the mind is to seek solutions, even when it's focused on the problems. By rooting around for a mature inquiry to your problems, you may discover solutions even before consulting the Tarot. Forming questions is like brainstorming. You will use wordplay, introspection, and creativity to craft an inquiry that the Tarot can clearly address.

Take time to contemplate the heart of the matter about which you are consulting the Tarot. If you are reading for others, you should encourage them to do the same. You may need to ask your querent (the person for whom you are reading) about details of her life in order to assist her with framing questions.

It is best to ask specific questions that lead to meaningful dialogue. Here are a few suggestions followed by poor examples of inquiry.

- **Good:** "May I please have clarification as to my boyfriend's feelings about our relationship?"
  Poor: "Is my boyfriend cheating on me?"

- **Good:** "Can you show me which career option is ideal for my greatest growth and success?"
  Poor: "Which job will get me the most money?"

- **Good:** "What process will my daughter go through to be happy and healthy?"
  Poor: "Will my daughter ever get off drugs?"

Do you see how the first examples offer an opening for narration and dialogue? Frame your question in such a way that it allows the Tarot to offer potential solutions, growth, and understanding. This will provide a richer, more mature experience.

Some good ways to phrase questions are:

- What is it about _____ that is for my highest and best good?

- What lessons can I learn from _____?

- How will _____ make me grow and become a better person?

Notice the tone of these examples is positive. It's a good idea to keep the framework of your inquiries upbeat and in the affirmative. Negative tones tend to result in a weak reflection in the cards.

When you formulate a question, hold that inquiry in your heart and mind as you touch, shuffle, and cut the cards. If you are reading for someone else, request your querent also hold the question in his/her consciousness. You may want to have your querent lay hands on the cards while directing the energy of the question to the Tarot. Focusing on the question will impress the Tarot with your earnest intent, thus reflecting more accurate outcomes in your reading.

It may take a little practice getting skilled at framing useful questions for the Tarot. That's okay. The Tarot is a labyrinth of self-discovery and illumination. The more you work with the Tarot, the more you will diversify in self-knowledge and maturity. Your skill in the art of using the Tarot will become a revealing and satisfactory process. Just be patient with yourself and follow your intuitive instincts.

193

GETTING ANSWERS WITH THE TAROT

By now, you have a good idea about framing mature questions and how card positions interact to answer your inquiries. You also have a basic understanding about the structure of the Tarot, how to handle the cards, and how your intuition is essential to the process of reading the cards.

The Tarot is a sophisticated network of symbols and meanings. This network is comprised of a diverse range of cultural perspectives. The Tarot also illustrates the complexity of the human experience in all its phases. With so many cultural and human angles to consider, it makes sense that the answers you uncover with the Tarot will be multi-faceted.

Responses from the Tarot are expressed on many different levels. This is a purposeful design. A multi-layered result will offer you many different views and options. Initially, you may find this confusing or frustrating. Perhaps you expect crystal clear "yes" or "no" answers from the Tarot. The Tarot will absolutely guide you in a direction and offer insight about your life, but it will not tell you in pat, hard-line terms.

How many times have you gotten a clear-cut, absolute answer to a question about the one-and-only correct path to take in life? Odds are, you haven't. This is because life is replete with variables.

If you move one way, your destiny shifts and creates other opportunities that might prove good or bad for you. There is no such thing as a rock-solid, absolute guarantee. Life is a twisty path, and your Tarot results will reflect the winding ways of living it.

To discern the different byways the Tarot discloses in a reading, it's helpful to know there are internal and external facets reflected in the cards. There is the inner life you live which deals with your thoughts and emotions. Then there is the outer life comprised of your friends, family, your home, your job, etc.

TAKING THE TWO-STEP APPROACH

When seeking answers, take a two-step approach. First, survey the cards with a goal to uncover inner aspects of yourself (or your querent). On this first pass, your intuition will be looking for insight into your thoughts and feelings. What kind of emotional upheaval or cleansing can be revealed in the cards? Contemplate the cards before you and try to identify an overarching theme about your emotional condition. Do the same for the inner world of thought. The cards will reflect what is foremost in your mind. Some of these reflections will be conscious thoughts, others will be unconscious. The

Tarot can serve up uncanny revelations about hidden thoughts (unconscious) that may be inhibiting your progress in life.

Exploring your inner life with the Tarot may expose truths you don't want to face. Be gentle with yourself, and know that the truth can set you free. The Tarot can offer emotional closure by revealing thoughts and feelings you may have overlooked or ignored. Realize that getting unstuck in your inner life will consequently get things flowing in your outer life.

When reading for others, you can still take a two-step approach. Although everyone's inner worlds are different, you can interpret thoughts and feelings when reading for other people. The first pass at the cards will reveal your querent's foremost thoughts and feelings. Be gentle in describing what you are seeing in the cards. Ask your querent questions to see if your interpretations are on the right track. For example, the Nine of Swords often indicates sleepless nights due to worry and fear. Ask your querent if she is grappling with deep concerns. Confirm whether her worries are causing her restlessness. Take a look at the other cards for emotional tips on how your querent can cope with her consuming worries.

Now take a second pass at the cards with intent to explore your external life. This perspective will uncover aspects about the people in your life and your environment. See if you can discern commonality in the cards. For example, if you have a lot of wands in your spread, this should prompt you to look at your creativity and/or social activities. You might see grievances with people that require forgiveness. Perhaps the cards are telling you to be more creative or get out and mingle more. Likewise, a predominance of Pentacles in a reading will expose aspects concerning money, home, and material matters.

The following is an example of how to take a two-step (inner and outer) approach to a reading. These cards were pulled randomly, with no particular question in mind. When cards are pulled casually like this, the answers you get will reveal the current status of your inner and external energies.

First Pass: The Inner World:

The Sword suit is all about thoughts, so you know you're dealing with an overarching theme of mental preoccupation with two Swords present. Cups represent emotion, and particularly matters of love. These cards suggest a theme that the mind is consumed by worrisome thoughts concerning love and/or close relationships.

Looking at the cards individually, we can narrow down that theme and start to get clear answers about the inner life. The Five of Swords represents an element of selfishness or entitlement. The figure takes for his own gain, and causes mental damage to those in his life as a result. There is a sense of cold calculation and a lack of remorse about his actions. The Seven of Swords accentuates and confirms this. Here again, we see a figure who is taking ideas from the community and running away without thought

to others. He is essentially turning his back on his village. The Six of Cups is a card that deals with relationships. It often implies repairing friendships or family connections that have been severed in the past. It suggests a longing for simplicity, understanding, and healing.

In summary, these cards indicate the inner life is consumed with regret over selfish thoughts and behaviors. It implies the inner desire to be fair, express love, and communicate (Six of Cups). However, the steely edges of a sharp (sword-like) mentality prohibit love and healing from taking place. The cards point out a cold, inflexible mind (Swords), and the emotional desire to be understood and be loved (Cups).

Second Pass: Outer World:

The Five of Swords indicates taking from friends or family. Perhaps an idea was stolen without credit given. This card may also signify loved ones leaving—a trip, relocation, or transition. While gone, they leave responsibilities behind for someone else to take care of. The Six of Cups suggests a chance to meet someone which leads to a blossoming relationship. This may be a rekindling of an old flame, or reconnecting with childhood friends. This card also represents service. An opportunity to serve the community—particularly through creative skills is also represented in this card. The Seven of Swords indicates moving away from the community. It implies gathering information and taking that knowledge elsewhere. This card often indicates a selfish motivation, or being secretive about plans to move on.

In summary, these cards indicate the outer world is challenged by relationships. The Sword cards express a "lone wolf" feel, yet the Cups card indicates social harmony. These cards indicate a need for healthy relationships, and establish an admirable standing in the community. However, selfishness or inappropriate action inhibits fulfillment of social desires.

Do you see how the inner world reading deals with only thoughts and emotions? The outer world reading is geared to illustrate what's going on with the external environment.

Different cards will reveal different issues. For example, the Tower card may indicate a crumbling of a belief system in the inner world. In the outer world, the Tower may indicate physical problems with health or home, or a need to rebuild physical structures.

Whether you are conducting an inner or outer evaluation, try not to freeze up from the complexity shown in the cards. Viewing a dozen cards in front of you might seem confusing because there is so much going on, so much to analyze.

Take a deep breath, loosen your mind, and be open to seeing the "big picture" the Tarot is offering you. Sitting with the cards in a relaxed state will prompt your intuition to discern patterns and themes. Once you can grasp an overall theme, you can fill in the details by exploring the cards individually.

Getting answers with the Tarot can be rewarding and enlightening. This book will help you with fundamental meanings, but the real excitement begins when you unlock your intuition and start exploring the multiple levels of insight the Tarot offers.

DOING READINGS

So far, this book has covered the basics on prepping your deck, priming your intuition, and cultivating a perfect question. Now it's time to do some readings!

To get you on the fast-track, run through this check-list to ensure all your basics are covered for a successful reading.

- **Prepare yourself.** Get in a relaxed, meditative state. This gets your intuition flowing. Also consider saying a small prayer or words of devotion to open up your heart and get good energy moving.

- **Prepare your environment.** Consider playing soothing music, lighting a candle, or burning some pleasing incense. These measures will enhance your intuition and your reading.

- **Prepare your deck.** See the "Handling the Cards" section for suggestions on charging and purifying your deck before you do a reading.

Once you and your deck are ready, it's time to start the reading! Here's a quick run-down for selecting and placing the cards for reading.

1. **Select a spread.** You may start with a simple three card reading or a more complicated lay-out. The spread you use will determine where you place the cards. This will determine how you read the cards, too.

2. **Formulate a question.** The "How to Ask Questions with Tarot" section will help you with this. Once you have a question, focus on it as you hold the cards in your hands.

3. **Shuffle.** Keep your question in your mind as you shuffle the cards.

4. **Cut.** With your question still keen in your focus, lay the cards face down and cut the deck. If you are reading for someone else, you may ask your querent to make the cut. It is customary to cut the deck three times, but the choice is yours.

5. **Spread the cards.** Collect the cuts and place the deck face down in one stack. Now with one hand spread out the cards like a fan.

6. **Pull.** Still focusing on your question, pull the cards one by one and place them face down in the positions of your spread. The order in which you pull the cards is dependent upon the type of spread you are using. Typically, cards are pulled and laid out from left to right then top to bottom. If you are reading for someone else, you may ask your querent to pull the cards as he/she focuses on the question.

7. **Place.** If you just want to lay cards out and see what happens, put the first card you pull in the center. This card is called the "significator;" it represents you (or your querent). The second card you pull will go to the left of your center (self) card. The third will go to the right. Further cards can be laid from top to bottom of your significator card.

8. **Flip.** Once you have all your cards in place, begin to turn them over. Do this in the same order you laid out the cards—from left to right, top to bottom. If you have a center (significator) card, flip that one over first.

Now that you have all these beautiful cards laid out before you, it's time to take a deep breath and calmly consider the cards. Once you've taken it all in, here's what you do:

1. What are some details that jump out at you first? Make a note of the things that capture your attention.

2. Identify the Major Arcana cards (if any) in the spread. Remember, these cards represent big issues in your life.

3. Next, ponder the Minor Arcana cards. Are there a lot of court cards? Are there more Pentacles in the spread than any other suit? Asking yourself these questions will get your intuition in sync with what the cards are telling you.

4. Pay attention to the colors of the cards. If you see a lot of yellow in the lay out, consider how that color makes you feel. Is it a happy color scheme, or a gloomy one?

5. Be mindful of what the characters in the cards are doing, and how they interact with the other cards. For example, you may see a Knight next to the Fool card. Maybe it looks like the Knight is charging at the Fool. This might remind you of that old saying "only fools rush in" which might be a word of caution relating to the query you posed to the cards.

Remember, the cards you pull respond to the meaning of the position in which it is placed. For example, a card drawn and placed in the center (significator) position represents you and where you are in your life right now.

Take your time with the cards. Pour over them with an open heart and mind. There's no pressure to reading the cards because there is no absolute right or wrong way to do it!

READING FOR OTHERS RESPONSIBLY

Doing readings can be tons of fun, especially if you are reading for your friends or family. It can also be an incredibly healing and rewarding experience. That said, there are a few important things to keep in mind when you are reading for others.

You and your querent may uncover some very intimate, private details in a reading. Be sure to handle these details maturely and with compassion. It's important to make your querent feel comfortable, safe, and supported during a reading. It's also a good idea to keep private matters confidential.

Be mindful of how you word your readings. For example, pulling the "Death" card and telling your querent she is going to die is simply unacceptable! This kind of thoughtless response will reflect poorly on you, and could cause irreparable damage to your querent. Be sensitive when conducting a reading for someone.

Above all else, follow the Tarot practitioner's creed: "Do no harm." Following this motto will keep you on the right track whether you read for yourself or others.

THE 4 BASIC SPREADS

BASIC SPREAD #1:
PAST, PRESENT, FUTURE

Three-card spreads are one of the most basic layouts, and are commonly used for quick answers.

The three-card spread shown below is known as a "Past, Present, Future" spread. It is used to discern outcomes of actions that influence the timing of events.

Past   Present   Future

Past and present timeframes are typically expressed in months. Months are revealed in the number of the Tarot card. For example, the Nine of Pentacles in the past position equates to events that took place nine months ago. Likewise, the Three of Wands expresses three months into your future in the sample shown on the next page. Timeframes for Major Arcana cards are determined by the card's position in the Major Arcana. For example, The Hierophant is the fifth card in the Major Arcana, and therefore represents 5 months. You can pre-assign different timeframes if you wish by changing the month delineation to days, weeks, or years.

To execute this reading, pull three cards and place them in past, present, and future positions (from left to right). The cards you draw in response to your intent or question should open a dialogue about what has happened in the past, what's going on right now, and what may happen in the future. This spread will show you consequences of your actions. It will also reveal what is delaying or speeding up your progress regarding your question.

To demonstrate how this reading works, a sample question is provided followed by sample cards pulled in response. Below the three-card spread are potential explanations and interpretations for the sample inquiry.

Keep in mind, these are only examples. Your interpretations will be different because your unique experience will influence the meaning of the cards.

SAMPLE INQUIRY

Dana is a professional secretary. She is concerned about work because she feels she can't advance in the job she's in right now. She wants to express her many talents, but feels her job doesn't allow this. She has been thinking about taking a new job or going into a different line of work. Travel has always appealed to her, and she's thought about being a travel agent. However, the job market is unstable, and she is fearful of relinquishing the good job she has now. Her question is: "What are some outcomes of my choices about my career?"

DANA'S PAST, PRESENT, FUTURE SPREAD

Past   Present   Future

Past (Nine of Pentacles)

Pentacles are materialistic cards. The Nine of Pentacles can easily resemble Dana and her desires to gain more wealth and growth at work. Consider the lushly dressed figure amongst a bountiful crop of grapes. These symbolize a need for creative expression and an environment within which to flourish. The falcon in the card confirms Dana's need to "hunt down" something satisfying for herself. As this is a timing spread, the nine indicates Dana started her ruminations about new opportunities nine months in the past. Her dreams for better career opportunities are big, beautiful, and promising according to this card.

CHANGING THE PAST

Ever wish you could change the past? You don't need a time machine to go back and mend fences. Time is a fluid, shifting thing. It's not linear like the timelines we see in history books. The past is just as flexible and adjustable as the future. You can influence your past (and therefore your future) by going back in time in your mind. Consider the card in the "Past" position for guidance about how to better approach grievances in your past. Then, get in a thoughtful, meditative state. Revisit the past, and use the Tarot as a guide to repair old mistakes. Make an effort to re-approach people or events that require healing. Doing this past-healing practice in your heart and mind is an energetic practice. Time is energy. The energy you invest in repairing past upsets will influence your present and future. Give it a try!

Present (The Lovers)

This is a Major Arcana card, so it indicates Dana is dealing with a karmic theme right now. This card indicates her passion for service at work will be a lifelong pursuit.

The Lovers is a partnership card, therefore it implies Dana is in a perfect position to establish important relationships at work. Because it's a Major Arcana card, it is likely that the business partnerships Dana establishes now will remain supportive in powerful and long-term ways. These business relationships are going to be key to Dana's advancement opportunities at work.

The archangel on the card implies higher guidance available to Dana right now. She may not be aware of it, but she has a loving spiritual guide that can positively influence her work decisions. She should take time to meditate and communicate with her "guardian angel" for advice about work.

Consider the male and female with the mountain between them. The opposing genders confirms Dana's opposing thoughts about staying at her job, or pursuing a different career. The mountain in the middle is her doubt and fear of the unknown which blocks her from making a choice. Dana should be reminded that The Lovers is a highly promising and beneficial card. In her present state, she should be encouraged to make a choice that enhances her well-being. She is in a prime position to make a move that supports her, makes her feel harmonious, and satisfies her passion.

Future
(Three of Wands)

The Three of Wands reveals what the next three months hold for Dana concerning the outcome of career choices. This card often implies staying grounded while letting others go out into the world and explore new vistas of life. This does not necessarily mean Dana will be stuck at the same job while watching others move forward.

As a predictive tool, the Future card can help Dana make educated choices about her career. Here are a few suggestions:

Let's say Dana pursued her dream to be a travel agent. What does the Future card say about that? The figure in the Three of Wands is standing on higher ground, overseeing ships in the distance. This indicates Dana may be supervising the travel of others. This dovetails with her desire to be a travel agent.

What if Dana decided to stay at her current job? The ships in the Three of Wands are symbolic of movement and exploration. The figure stays home (at the same job) while wistfully watching opportunity sail by. In this light, the card suggests she may always have a longing for what could have been.

The suit of Wands deals with creativity, passion, and things that ignite enthusiasm. In this case, the Three of Wands is an encouragement for Dana to follow her dream. The figure in the Three of Wands has his back turned. This may indicate Dana must turn her back on things that keep her in her comfort zone. The figure is gripping one of the wands while two are at his back. This is a message for Dana that says, "Hold tightly to that which inspires you. You will always have support backing your creative endeavors."

Whatever Dana decided, looking back at the Nine of Pentacles and The Lovers there is a sense of positivity and support. They confirm that whatever choice Dana makes, she will have the insight and backing that will put her on top like the man seen in the Three of Pentacles.

CHANGE YOUR FUTURE

Don't like what the cards reveal about your future? Change it! The future is a very changeable thing. One or two small actions or attitude adjustments can change your future in big ways. Keep this in mind as you go through your days, months, and years. Work to inject positive elements in your life. Adding more kindness and positivity in your daily actions accumulates over time to create a brighter future.

BASIC SPREAD #2:
DAILY ENCOUNTER

The Daily Encounter Reading is a spread you can do for yourself at the beginning of the day. This spread is particularly helpful because it gives you an inside track about your day. Forewarned is forearmed. If you see foreboding or disturbing cards in this spread, then be conscious of it and make corrective adjustments throughout your day.

You   What you encounter   Outcome
                     today

The "You" card is the signifier, so it represents you. It reflects your energetic tone at the moment of pulling the card. The center "Encounter" card indicates what kind of joys, fun, people, surprises, events, and/or conflicts you may encounter on this day. The "Outcome" card reflects how your day will conclude. Be mindful of this outcome card because it may show you how to handle conflict more effectively. If the "Outcome" card feels negative to you, then you might want to focus on lessons you can learn from the day's experiences.

This Daily Encounter spread is a progression, with each card relating to each other. You will build a story from left to right. This means the "You" card plays a part in what you experience in the day ("What You Encounter"). Likewise, the "You" and "Encounter" card will influence the "Outcome" card. Try to see connections between these three cards. Think of one card as a consequence of another.

When you pull the cards for the spread, place them in order from left to right.

SAMPLE THREE-CARD DAILY ENCOUNTER SPREAD

So, let's say your question is: "What lessons can I learn from this day?"

You

What you encounter today

Outcome

You (The Fool reversed)

This may be a quick and easy spread, but that doesn't make the Fool card any less weighty in its meaning. The Fool is a Major Arcana card. As such, this represents major issues you repeatedly deal with throughout your life.

The Fool is symbolic of experiencing the wonders of life with childlike abandon. It also indicates a zeal for new beginnings and adventure. Reversed, it suggests you might not subscribe to this approach. Perhaps you struggle with a negative outlook about life.

As a daily read, you are ideally pulling these cards at the beginning of your day. The reversed Fool may indicate new beginnings are a source of frustration for you. Maybe you've never been a morning person, and dread the start of each day.

The reversed Fool has an "up in the air" energy. It implies lack of structure, confusion, and disorganization. Take these issues into consideration with regard to who you are and how you approach your day. Be honest with yourself and recognize the reversed Fool might point out character flaws that prohibit progress.

Outcome (Ace of Wands)

Your day may have had an unsavory tone, but the Ace of Wands offers hope. Wands are a suit of creativity, passion, and social stimulation. Aces are symbolic of taking initiative and action.

GET AN ATTITUDE ADJUSTMENT!

The "You" position can give a revealing outlook into your emotional, mental, and physical status. Pay close attention to this card. Think of ways you can enhance your attitude, or improve it if the "You" card appears unsettling. Remember, YOU are the ultimate master of your daily outcomes. A positive attitude is often the single most important factor in turning your day from sad to glad!

What You Encounter Today (Eight of Swords)

Swords are the suit of mental energy. This card indicates you struggle with defeating thoughts. This may be connected to the theme of the reversed Fool, meaning a poor attitude or disorganized approach to life may lead to negative thoughts throughout your day.

These negative thoughts cause you to feel helpless and stuck. This interpretation comes from the figure in the Eight of Swords being bound and blindfolded. Be aware of disabling thoughts throughout your day. Your thoughts might not be the only culprit in feeling bound. Other people or circumstances may force you into thinking you have no course of action. Consequently, be mindful of potential problems in people or events that you might be able to avoid. Now that you are aware of this potential snafu, you can take corrective action so you can avoid getting tied up in a negative situation.

As a future-telling card, the Ace of Wands indicates you are compelled to change the course of your day to the positive. It implies you have the power at hand to take charge of your situation. The Ace of Wands is also a card of bright ideas. You may receive inspiration when you take action in the affirmative. Seeking creative solutions throughout the day will render beneficial outcomes. Counteract negativity by tapping into something that ignites your passion. Consider initiating a social outing to uplift your mood. Call a friend or go to lunch with someone you love. Odds are you're going to get a blessing when you take positive action as the Ace of Wands advises.

TURN A NEGATIVE INTO A POSITIVE

If you pull a card that looks unpleasant, don't freak out! It doesn't mean you're going to encounter a bad experience in your day. Rather than revert to an "oh no! What's going to befall me!" attitude, try approaching a negative card with a positive attitude. You can even pull an additional card on top of the card that concerns you to get ideas and solutions about how to approach a potentially uncomfortable situation in your day.

UNEXPECTED PLEASURES

Like surprises? Modify this spread to help you create some pleasant, serendipitous moments in your day. Simply add a card placement to this spread that represents "Happy Surprises I Can Expect in My Day." This position is great for reinforcing your psyche with the idea you can create your reality. The card you lay down in this position can influence how you approach your day, too. It's kind of like setting a positive intention. For example, if you see a happy card like the Ten of Cups, you're going to expect some wonderful things to pop into your day. Remember, expectation is half of manifesting what you want in life!

BASIC SPREAD #3:
TAKE ACTION

This four-card spread is good to use when you need a little help making a decision or taking action.

You   Known   Unknown   Action

The "You" card is the significator. It represents you (or your querent) and where you are right now. The "Known" card reveals issues about which you have solid information. This is the known quantity in your life. These are facts of which you are aware. The "Unknown" card addresses people, situations, or events that are influencing your situation, but you are *not* aware of them. These are factors working behind the scenes that can help or hinder your direction. The "Action" card reveals the best course of action to take in your situation. It should help clarify the right choice to make regarding your issue.

Weigh the interpretations between "Known" and "Unknown" against each other. See how these factors play a role for your best interests. The "You" card in relation to the other cards helps you understand whether you are willing or unwilling to make the right choice.

If the "Unknown" is too disturbing, or the "You" card clearly indicates you're not ready to make a move, consult the "Action" card for clarification. The "Action" card can point you in the right direction, or it may give you ideas about why you're not ready to take action.

SAMPLE INQUIRY

Marla just graduated from high school. She feels overwhelmed by the choices she is faced with. She feels like the world is her oyster; there are so many opportunities! She has scholarships for college lined up, but she also has resources to take a year off to travel Europe. She's considered working for her father's graphic design company, as this also seems appealing. She is frustrated because she wants to make the best choice. Marla's question is: "Should I go to college, or should I take a year off to work or travel?"

MARLA'S TAKE ACTION SPREAD

| You | Known | Unknown | Action |

You (Four of Cups)

The suit of Cups deals with emotion, dreams, and intuition. It indicates the condition of our feelings and offers suggestions on how to purify our emotional state. Marla is dealing with emotional choices about her future dreams. The Four of Cups confirms several options in front of Marla. These option are indicated by the three cups lined up before the figure in the card. There is, however, one choice that will be ideal for her. This is illustrated by the cup floating in front of the figure.

213

Notice the figure's crossed arms and legs. This implies Marla's emotions are blocked. This is thwarting her ability to see the right choice to make. The figure is also sitting in what appears to be a contemplative state. This may hint to taking more time to meditate on choices with a goal to get emotional clarity about the right path.

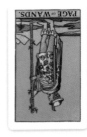

Unknown (Page of Wands reversed)

Upright, this card is a good omen for travel and creative pursuits. But the card is reversed, so there are influences that Marla isn't aware of that put the kibosh on travel prospects.

Known (Seven of Wands)

Wands deal with creativity, community, and inspiration. This card further confirms that Marla is fully aware of all the options available to her. Look at the wands jabbing up at the figure from the foreground. This suggests many different people or opportunities poking at Marla. The figure is standing on higher ground in a defensive position. This symbolizes that Marla knows she is standing in a good position no matter what choice she makes. However, she feels like she has to defend her choices to others, or justify her actions to herself.

The reversed Page of Wands also sends a message of taking the easy way out. It represents laziness and resting on one's laurels. It confirms that Marla is very talented, and able to do whatever she wants. However, knowing that might tempt Marla to not apply herself. Subconsciously, Marla may want to take the easy way rather than work hard for results. For example, she may be considering working for her dad's company because she knows it's comfortable and easier than going to college.

A reversed card in this position often points to self-sabotaging behaviors. As the reader, consider gently talking to Marla about her motivations for her three options. What motivates her to stay, go to school, or go abroad? She may have an unconscious desire to staunch her growth by choosing the comfortable path. You may also want to encourage Marla to question why she wants to travel. Maybe travel is a way to run away from responsibility; she may not be aware of that motivation.

CONQUERING FEAR

Afraid of the unknown? Join the club! Everybody gets a little edgy when it comes to unknown elements in life. But that doesn't mean we have to live in fear. This spread can help you face your uneasiness about the hidden factors of life. Forewarned is forearmed!

Action
(Three of Pentacles)

This card clearly points to work and showing off skills. Pentacles are about money, materialism, and putting our dreams into reality. The number three is a highly creative number. In essence, this card is about working in a creative environment. It suggests putting skills to work in order to establish a solid foundation for the future. In Marla's example, it seems working for her dad would be the most fitting course of action. However, college is hard work, too. It requires utilizing talents to establish an educational foundation. This Pentacle card does not hint to any kind of travel, so Marla's idea to go abroad might have to be put on the backburner for the time being.

Additionally, the Three of Pentacles addresses self-confidence. Looking back on her Significator card (Four of Cups), you can see Marla might lack the faith in herself to make the right decision. In response, the Three of Pentacles suggests Marla gets to work on her self-esteem so she can confidently make the right choice for her best outcome.

TAKE A MOMENT

Be sensible about actions you take. Remember that every action in life has a consequence. If after doing this spread you are still unsure about what you should do, the best action to take might be nothing at all. Sometimes sleeping on it, or just waiting a bit is the best solution. You may find after a little pause, the next time you perform this spread the cards will be much clearer and you'll feel better about your next step.

BASIC SPREAD #4:
THE MODIFIED CROSS

This is a modified version based on the traditional Celtic Cross spread. You can use this for any issue or question you have for the cards. This spread will help you understand what's holding you back and it will offer clarification about your issues.

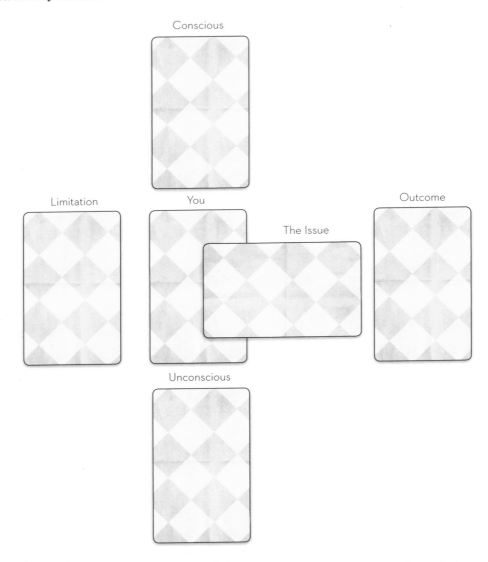

Pull the cards and place them face up in the following order:

1. You
2. Issue (crossing card)
3. Conscious
4. Unconscious
5. Limitation
6. Outcome

The "You" position is the significator. It represents you (or your querent) and your present-moment energy.

The crossing "Issue" card represents the crux of an issue you're dealing with at this moment. It could be a true conflict, or it could be something beneficial like an upcoming wedding or vacation.

The crowning "Conscious" card represents the things you have control over in the situation. It can also represent things you might be over-controlling. This card reveals the level of your awareness about the "Issue." The "Conscious" card may also help mold your thoughts. For example, if you have a negative attitude about the "Issue" the "Conscious" card might help you modify your thoughts in a better direction.

The "Unconscious" card will reveal your hidden thoughts and feelings about the "Issue." It may expose hidden agendas or motivations. For example, you may be sabotaging yourself and not even be aware of it. The "Unconscious" card will explain the hidden truths about your thoughts and behavior.

The "Limitation" card represents a potential snag in your plans concerning the "Issue" card. This may be someone or something in your past that tripped you up or impedes your progress.

The far right "Outcome" card sums up the story told in the spread. It should offer a conclusion or reveal the appropriate action to take about the issue. It also shows how your conscious and unconscious life influences the results of your issue.

SAMPLE INQUIRY

Dan is having relationship problems. He feels flummoxed about women, and he doesn't understand why all his relationships fail. He claims to be generous and attentive. Yet it seems every time he makes a move for an exclusive commitment, his partners always pull away. Dan's question is: "What is it about me and my behavior that pushes potential partners away?"

DAN'S MODIFIED CROSS SPREAD

Conscious

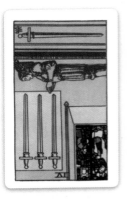

Limitation

You

The Issue

Outcome

Unconscious

You (King of Pentacles reversed)

This card represents Dan, and it confirms he is indeed in a position to be generous with his resources. Kings are typically men of power and authority and have diverse assets at their command. However, the card is reversed which indicates an inappropriate or dysfunctional use of power. The women in Dan's life may easily recognize his assets. However, as the relationship progresses, Dan may express tendencies to be overbearing or controlling. This may contribute to women pulling away from him.

Pentacles have a physical undertone. If Dan shows signs of being domineering, women may subconsciously expect Dan to become physically abusive. Or, if not physically abusive, Dan might want to control a woman's material aspects. He may want to dress her a certain way, or buy her things to win her love. These behaviors are often interpreted as a man compensating for some kind of lack in his life. The women with whom Dan is trying to form relationships may see right through these behaviors and want to avoid getting tangled with him.

The Issue (Five of Cups)

This is a great confirmation of what Dan said in his consultation. Cups often deal with emotional issues, especially love. The figure in the card shows a posture of feeling bereft of all hope. Before him are tipped cups which symbolize several failed attempts at making a loving, emotional connection. There are, however, two cups left standing upright. This implies there is hope for Dan's love life. The figure has his back turned. This suggests Dan is focused on the failure (the tipped cups) and has a hard time focusing on the promise of love available to him.

Conscious (Four of Swords reversed)

Swords rule the realm of thought and mind. In a reversed position, this card is symbolic of holding onto harmful thoughts. The figure is stone-cold, and is always faced with the sharp edge of unfavorable thoughts. This reversed card often points to dwelling in judgment and carrying grudges. He may not want to admit it, but this card reveals Dan is conscious of his feelings of resentment. He knows he is harboring resentment towards women because they don't seem to accept him for who he is. These multiple grudges against past partners have built up within Dan, and he recognizes this is a barrier for future progress.

Unconscious (Six of Pentacles)

As mentioned, the suit of Pentacles deals with materialism and value. The Six of Pentacles is about giving in kind, philanthropic ways. It's also a card of balance, as illustrated by the scales in the card. This balance is brought about by seeing lack in the world and filling that void through charitable compassion. In this position, the Six of Pentacles gives insight into Dan's unconscious thoughts and behavior. As such, Dan might be aware that he is a man of means, but he does *not* realize he has the ability to give unconditionally.

In essence, Dan isn't aware that he can strike a balance between his need for control and his partner's need to feel equal. He is also unaware that women want to love Dan for who he is, not for what material items he can give. He doesn't realize that his generosity may be an attempt to dominate women or control the relationship. Revealing this unconscious aspect within Dan may encourage him to reform his control issues. His heart has the capability of giving value to women with no strings attached. He just needs to recognize this.

Limitation (The Magician)

This is a Major Arcana card, so it has huge import. The Magician is about utilizing resources with a goal to reach full potential and work wonders in life. Because it's a Major Arcana card, this theme runs through Dan's life time and time again. In the "Limitation" position, Dan may feel unable to embrace his potential in a balanced, healthy way.

You've already seen in previous cards that Dan uses his resources for control in relationships. The Magician allows his resources to work for him; he doesn't use them to manipulate others. Dan's limitation may be a false belief that his power lies in his wealth or resources rather than his heart and emotional assets. As a Major (karmic) card, this issue is going to consistently undermine Dan's attempts at obtaining true love. Dan must come to terms with this limiting belief if there is to be any hope of a lasting, healthy relationship.

Outcome (Three of Cups)

You can see the frivolity and fun in this card. Remember, cups are associated with love and emotion. Therefore, on the surface, this card implies Dan's outcome will be one of love and happiness. The ripened fruit in the card suggests Dan's emotions have matured, and he is now able to harvest a healthy relationship. It's important for Dan to realize his outcome is contingent upon self-nurturing and tending to the garden of his emotions. At the very least, Dan will be in a position to meet new potential partners, and his experience will be joyful. At the most, Dan's forecast for love looks very promising.

GOING OLD SCHOOL

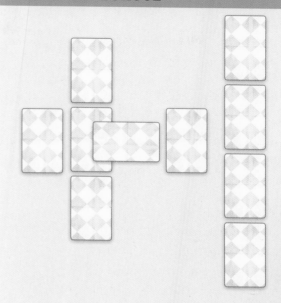

This is a modified cross spread because it excludes four other positions typically seen in the traditional Celtic cross spread. You can go old school and add four positions along the right-hand side of this modified cross. The additional positions, from top to bottom are: **Your Attitude** (how you feel about the crossing card, **Outside Influences** (external factors that effect your situation), **Hopes and Fears** (things you wish or dread happening about your issue), and **Summary** (this sums up the whole reading of the spread—it's like a wrap-up for your reading).

CONSCIOUS AND UNCONSCIOUS

Confused about "conscious" and "unconscious"? The term *conscious* is Latin, and it means "awake, aware, or knowing." *Unconscious* is, therefore, the opposite of that. When interpreting these cards, take into account that your mind is a multi-faceted, diverse universe. You are a unique being with amazing complexity. These cards can reveal deep, profound aspects of your beautiful self.

SPREADS FOR SPECIFIC QUESTIONS

FINANCIAL FORECAST SPREAD

You've probably had your share of financial ups and downs. It's no secret that money (making it and losing it) is transitional by nature. Sometimes you've got it, sometimes you don't.

Considering the cyclical behavior of money, this Financial Forecast spread is great at pinning down the transitions your money is making. This spread can forecast the highs and lows you can expect in your financial status.

The spread positions are based on the four quarters of a fiscal year. As such, it's best to do this reading for yourself at the beginning of the year. January is always a good time to do any kind of reading in which you want a view of what's going to happen in the upcoming year.

The four quarters of the year are broken into three months per quarter like so:

1st—January through March

2nd—April through June

3rd—July through September

4th—October through December

The cards drawn for each quarter will give you an inside track about what your money will do within these three-month brackets of time. You should read the activities in the quarters in chronological procession. The activities in the first quarter will influence the second quarter, and so on. You can draw relationships between the quarters to see how certain actions influence the flow of money. As you read this spread, see if you can find overarching themes and patterns.

HOW TO SET UP THE SPREAD

Pull the cards and place them face up in the following order:

1. You

2. First Quarter

3. Second Quarter

4. Third Quarter

5. Fourth Quarter

6. Outcome

You

1st Quarter 2nd Quarter 3rd Quarter 4th Quarter

Outcome

SAMPLE FINANCIAL FORECAST SPREAD

You

1st Quarter   2nd Quarter   3rd Quarter   4th Quarter

Outcome

The "You" card is the significator. It represents you and your overall response to monetary situations. This card illuminates some of your beliefs about money, too. Expect this card to reveal false beliefs about money as well as conscious and unconscious attitudes about your financial standing.

The "Outcome" card will give you insight as to corrective action to take about your finances. This card also sums up your financial outlook for the year.

This is a money-focused reading with a specific goal to take a look at your finances. As such, no question is required for the reading. However, as you handle and pull the cards *do* keep your intuition focused on the energy of money and how it can work for you.

SAMPLE SPREAD

You (Knight of Pentacles reversed)

The Knights of the Tarot realm are all about action. If reversed, action is stalled. Knights of Pentacles are the most plodding and methodical knights compared to their feisty counterparts. In the reversed position, this card suggests your ability to plan, manage, and take charge of your finances is not your forte. The horse in the Knight card is a sign of mobility and moving forward. The reversal implies setbacks, retroaction, and stagnation. The active energy of the Knight indicates your spirit is willing to do the work for financial gain, but the reversal implies challenges. The reversed Knight is a sign of false beliefs or blockages concerning your ideas about money.

1st Quarter (Eight of Pentacles)

The imagery of the card is clear. Hard work. Focus. Honing your skills in order to produce results. From January to March, you will find yourself buckling down to meet financial goals. This card is often a sign of manual, physical labor. You may need to invest sweat equity to gain headway. The pentacles are hung for display, this implies you may have an opportunity to show off your best assets. Perhaps you will be given the chance to impress investors. The pentacle laying beneath the figure's seat suggests you will make enough money in this quarter to "sit on" and put away for a rainy day. The home in the background implies money allotted for home improvements. Overall, you should experience a financial gain this quarter, but not without a lot of hard work.

2nd Quarter (Ten of Wands reversed)

This card deals with gathering resources and keeping a tight hold on them. Reversed, the card indicates a tendency to hoard. You may feel an urge to hold tightly to the gain you experienced in the 1st quarter. This card may also point to selfishness and greediness. Wands are in the realm of creativity and passion. In this quarter you will learn that hoarding will cause your creativity and joy to suffer. The figure's back is turned, which suggests you may turn your back on financial partners and/or investors. This may entail taking your assets off the negotiation table or pulling your resources from a financial investment. The figure cannot see where he is going for all the wands blocking his view. This is a warning not to become blinded by your own self-centered motives.

4th Quarter (The Devil)

This is a Major Arcana card. As such, special attention should be paid because you are dealing with major life-altering events. These events tend to recur until you learn the life-lesson. The Devil represents anything that takes control of your life and puts you in emotional bondage. This could be an addiction like gambling which may be making you a slave to money. Or The Devil could represent business partners who keep you chained to a project you think is destined to fail. The Devil is also a neon sign for debt. This quarter may find you in the bondage of overspending and overindulgence.

3rd Quarter (Two of Cups)

The winged lion and caduceus are symbols of powerful healing and balance. This indicates you learned a few lessons from the 2nd quarter that got you back on track this quarter. The caduceus may also be an encouragement to look into the health industry for financial gain. The Two of Cups is a card of harmonious relationships. Consequently, you may encounter a healing in the last quarter which reestablished financial partnerships. As cups deal with intuition, you may find yours on fire this quarter. Follow your instinct, and go with your gut about financial investments. Doing so will ensure equilibrium for your pocket book. You will have support and establish healthy connections that will help your money matters. Overall, this quarter will be on the upswing.

Outcome (Six of Swords)

Interpretations of all four quarter cards indicate it's been a rocky year for you financially. The suit of Swords deals with the mind, and how your thoughts influence your life. With backs turned and heads down, the Six of Swords suggests a time of withdrawal and introspection about what you could have done differently in the financial year. The bowman in the card implies you still have mobility. It also suggests you certainly have the ability to navigate yourself out of rocky waters. The family in the boat may be a sign of moving your family to a better financial lot in life. The choppy waves on the right side of the boat opposed to the calm waters on the other side is a positive sign. It is an indication that you are moving out of turbulence into tranquil financial seas.

Use the Pentacles

Want to get laser-beam focus on your finances? Try using only the Pentacle cards in a reading. Before shuffling, pull out all the cards in the suit of Pentacles. Because Pentacles address material and money issues, reading with these cards exclusively can help you zero in on your money matters.

Use the Moon

Need quicker answers about your money matters? Try using this same Financial Forecast spread, but instead of using the annual quarters, use the phases of the moon. Assign card placements for the following positions: New Moon, First Quarter (half moon), Third Quarter (half moon), and Full Moon. The full cycle of the moon takes 27 to 29 days, which means you can get a glimpse of your financial forecast within the timeframe of a month instead of an annual overview.

Use a Single Card

The Tarot can be a great financial planner. Consider pulling just one card in response to your money-related question. The card you pull can offer advice and guidance about what financial action to take. Contemplate the card you pulled, and relate it to your question. Sometimes pulling one card for a quick answer can be the best way to square up your money concerns.

LOVE AND RELATIONSHIPS SPREAD

We all know love can be a complicated and mysterious thing. You can use this sample Tarot spread to clarify some questions or concerns you might have about your current love relationship.

For the sake of simplicity, "His, Him, and He" are used to identify your partner in this spread, but both genders are implied.

Pull the cards and place them face up in the following order:

1. Your partner
2. His attributes
3. His flaws
4. His inner thoughts about you
5. Your inner thoughts about Him
6. Strengths in the relationship
7. Weaknesses in the relationship
8. Potential for a healthy relationship
9. Potential roadblocks to a healthy relationship
10. Outcome/final analysis

"Your Partner" represents the person for whom you have affection. This could be a person you just starting dating, a long-term mate, or someone you might meet in the future. Be clear about which option you are seeking clarification about before the reading. Either way, this card represents the status of your partner's energy right now.

"His attributes" addresses defining characteristics that make your partner a great catch. These are assets you admire, he admires in himself, and are generally considered good qualities by others.

"His flaws" deals with quirks, foibles, and personality defects in your partner. These are deficits in character that cause problems for you, himself, and others.

"His inner thoughts about you" and "Your inner thoughts about him" can be intensely revealing cards. You may know how you feel about your mate, and vice versa. But sometimes we hide our innermost thoughts about someone. This is done for a myriad of reasons like self-protection, denial, or resistance to conflict. These cards show your innermost feelings about each other so you can get to the core truth.

His Attributes

Strengths in the Relationship

Outcome Final Analysis

Your Partner

His Inner Thoughts About You

Your Inner Thoughts About Him

Potential for a Healthy Relationship

Potential Problems or Roadblocks to Having a Healthy Relationship

His Flaws

Weaknesses in the Relationship

The "Potential for a healthy relationship" addresses precisely what the position implies. This card shows if there is a possibility for a long-term, harmonious partnership between you and your mate. If the card is unsavory, then explore the card meaning in more depth to determine the reason. You can also explore more reasons for negativity in this position by consulting the cards in the "Weaknesses in the relationship" and "Potential roadblocks to a healthy relationship" positions.

"Strengths in the relationship" and "Weaknesses in the relationship" are designed to show you what's working and what's not. After you interpret the cards in these positions, you can accentuate the positive and consciously work on the negatives.

"Potential roadblocks to a healthy relationship" is the crossing card. It exposes snafus and possible derailment in the partnership. This card can be essential in avoiding heartbreak. It is a predictive card, so it will foretell behavioral patterns or events in the future that will negatively affect your relationship.

The "Outcome/final analysis" card offers you a summary of the entire reading. It won't go so far as to say, "Yes, stick with this guy!" or tell you, "No way! Run!" But it *will* offer clues as to what ultimate choices you might make in navigating the relationship.

Because this is a love-specific spread, formulating a question to learn specifics about the relationship is optional. However, *do* keep your partner and your relationship in focus as you are handling and pulling the cards for this spread.

A common tendency for a new reader is to become overwhelmed with a large spread such as this one. So many different cards might be confusing. When approaching a big spread like this, take a deep breath and get an overall feel for the layout. Consider the overall color scheme of the spread. Happy colors? Gloomy colors? Take stock of the Major Arcana cards. Are there a lot of them? If so, you're dealing with big, karmic issues regarding love and relationships. These cards reveal profound themes you will encounter repeatedly throughout your life. What about the Minor Arcana? Is one suit represented more than another? If there are more swords than any other suit in the spread, you know you're dealing with a lot of mental energy.

SAMPLE LOVE AND RELATIONSHIPS SPREAD

His Attributes

Strengths in the Relationship

Outcome Final Analysis

Your Partner

His Inner Thoughts About You

Your Inner Thoughts About Him

Potential for a Healthy Relationship

Potential Problems or Roadblocks to Having a Healthy Relationship

His Flaws

Weaknesses in the Relationship

SAMPLE SPREAD

Your partner
(Eight of Cups)

Because Cups deal with deep emotion and intuition, your partner is likely very sensitive to the realm of feelings. There is a lot of water in the card which is symbolic of purification and emotional flow. Your partner may be in an emotional current and working to cleanse himself of emotional upheavals. Cups are also referred to as "love cards." Consider the position of the cups in relation to the figure in the card. The man is walking *away* from the cups. This suggests your partner may feel he needs to walk away from love or emotional issues to gain perspective. The moon symbolizes a desire to gain illumination through intuitive perception. It also indicates your partner may have a tendency to be influenced by outside forces.

His attributes
(Knight of Swords)

Knights carry an active, assertive, take-charge energy. One of the things you love about your mate is his ability to set his mind to a pursuit and move mountains to attain his vision. He is very strong-minded, and has no problem expressing his opinions. This Knight implies your mate enjoys upward mobility, and he excels in mental conquest.

His flaws
(Four of Pentacles)

Pentacles deal with material matters and things that represent value. Notice how the figure in the card holds his value close. Your partner may have a tendency to keep value to himself. The clutching of the pentacle indicates your partner might be stingy. He may not be very good at sharing his material resources. The card also signifies hoarding, greed, and selfishness.

His inner thoughts about you (The High Priestess reversed)

Because it's a Major Arcana card, the meaning of The High Priestess may reveal thoughts that other partners in your past or future may have had about you in addition to your current mate. The High Priestess is replete with mystery and covered in shadow. Reversed, that darkness is doubly so. This implies your mate may not truly understand you or why you do the things you do. Misunderstanding may also lead to mistrust. He is unsteady about his thoughts for you because he doesn't understand where you come from. The pillars in the card suggest he is of two minds about you. This leads him to get confused and impatient when he sets his mind upon figuring you out.

Your inner thoughts about him (Two of Swords)

Interestingly, the two crossed swords indicate you are of two minds about your mate as well. The crossed swords also suggest you feel defensive with your partner or feel you must defend your thoughts. The blindfold implies never quite seeing who your partner really is. You sense he does not show his true self, which means you have to rely on your intuition to get a read on what he's feeling. This is denoted by the moon (intuition) and water (feelings) in the card.

Strengths in the relationship (Knight of Wands)

To be sure, there is fire and passion between you two! This is an enthusiastic Knight and represents active creativity. You and your mate inspire each other. You both feed the fuel of your desires through your willingness to charge ahead into new creative adventures.

Weaknesses in the relationship (Seven of Cups reversed)

Where the Knight of Wands represents strength in creative diversity, it may also be a weakness. The Seven of Cups reversed represents being overwhelmed by too much choice. Too many emotions in the relationship may lead to exasperation. Always being "switched on" causes chaos to the point of being distracted from priorities in the relationship.

Potential for a healthy relationship (Ace of Cups)

This is a very auspicious card for love relationships. Aces are about new beginnings. If this is a new relationship, how you two treat each other in the beginning will set the stage for future promise. The Ace of Cups features the dove, which is symbolic of healing, compassion, and peace. As long as these beatitudes are kept in the forefront of your relationship, the signs are good for success.

Potential roadblocks to a healthy relationship (The Moon)

Since The Moon is a Major Arcana card, you may want to take a close look at this card for advice about deep, recurring emotional issues. The Moon presents varying degrees of complexity and possibility. It encourages reliance upon intuition and has a dreamy connotation. The Moon illuminates the darkness, but it cannot shine on its own. Your partnership must be equally yoked in order for you and your partner to be luminaries in love. The baying dogs in the card indicate conflict or disagreements caused by misunderstanding or confusion. This is confirmed by other cards previously interpreted. The Moon is also symbolic of timing. The timing in the different phases (when to date, when to meet the parents, when to marry, etc.) of your relationship may be vital to success.

Outcome/final analysis (The Hanged Man)

Another Major Arcana card, the influence of The Hanged Man will be felt for the duration of your relationship with this and possibly future partners. As an Outcome card, The Hanged Man sends a message of "wait and see what happens." The Hanged Man encourages suspending action or judgment before all the facts have presented themselves. He possesses a radiating halo which suggests you will come to a point of advanced clarity and positivity about the direction of your relationship.

Love spreads can be tricky to interpret because they deal with more than one person. It's not all about you. It's about you, your partner, and the relationship. The Tarot can give us insight into the people we love (or want to love us), but people can change over time, or even in an instant. Keep this in mind as you read your love spreads. You can even take the change factor into consideration by laying out an additional card. This extra card might represent something like "What are some changes in my partner that effect the relationship?" Place this extra card out to the side, to the right of the crossing card. This "change" card will reveal transitions and attitude adjustments your partner will experience that will have an influence on you and the partnership.

YOUR CUPS RUNNETH OVER

Does Cupid's arrow need a little better aim? Try using just the Cups cards for this spread. Because the suit of Cups deals with love and emotions, using these cards exclusively can ramp up your romantic forecasts. Before shuffling the cards, simply remove all cards that belong to the suit of Cups. Then shuffle and go about laying out the spread as instructed using only the Cups cards. You may find this method might be more revealing to matters of the heart.

WHOLE HEALTH REPORT SPREAD

This is a great spread to utilize when you want to get a "check up" on your health. This spread is holistic; it incorporates the three prime aspects of health: mind, body, and spirit.

Pull the cards and place them face up in the following order:

1. You
2. Mind
3. Body
4. Spirit
5. Corrective action for the mind
6. Corrective action for the body
7. Corrective action for the spirit

The "You" card is the significator. It represents you and offers an overall insight into your health status at this moment. This card reflects challenges you may know about, and a few you may not know.

The "Mind" card is a readout of what is going on in the realm of thought. It will pinpoint limiting thoughts as well as thoughts that serve you.

The "Body" card is a reflection of your physical status. Read properly, this card will confirm a few ailments, or it may confirm perfect health.

The "Spirit" card mirrors back your level of intuition. It will clue you in on aspects of your spiritual life that need work. It should also validate areas of your spirit that are active and functioning just fine.

All of the corresponding "Corrective Action" cards will serve as advice. These cards will give corrective guidance, or they will confirm you are on the right health-track.

This is not a predictive card spread; the reading will not forecast in the future. Rather, this is your biological read-out right *now*.

As this is a health-focused reading, a question pointed to the cards isn't necessary. However, you will want to funnel your focus about health matters into the cards so you can get the clearest response.

> Don't panic if you pull negative cards in any one position. As mentioned, the Tarot does not provide pat answers. Your job is to maturely interpret the cards, mining deeper meaning from each one. You can also consult the "Corrective Action" cards for further illumination about what's going on and what to do about it.

You

Mind

Body

Spirit

Corrective Action
for Mind

Corrective Action
for Body

Corrective Action
for Spirit

SAMPLE WHOLE HEALTH REPORT SPREAD

You

Mind

Body

Spirit

Corrective Action
for the Mind

Corrective Action
for the Body

Corrective Action
for the Spirit

SPECIFIC QUESTIONS

240

SAMPLE SPREAD

You (Strength reversed)

As a Major Arcana card, the message of Strength is a life-long factor for you. In an upright position, the Strength card illustrates confidence, patience, and poise as a source of strength. Reversed, it suggests a perversion of strength. This can mean employing power plays and a need for control in your life. Whether reversed or upright, this card deals with the battle between your animal (primal) self and your higher self. This means there is conflict between the flesh and the spirit. The reversed position implies your spirit is weak, and you are giving into your animal urges. This may mean giving into addictions that can damage your health. This reversed card indicates a need to dominate your mind, body, and spirit. However, taking control over health may manifest in abusive ways. It may also indicate weakness and a lack of discipline required to achieve optimum health.

Mind (Wheel of Fortune)

Round and round your mind goes! Where it stops, who knows? This is what the Wheel of Fortune card implies in this position. Although your mind may be filled to the brim with dizzying thoughts and ideas, you *do* have *some* focus. The Wheel of Fortune card represents deeper knowledge. Consider the four fixed signs in each corner of the card: Aquarius (Air), Scorpio (Water), Leo (Fire), and Taurus (Earth). Each of these characters consults an ancient text. This implies the mind craves knowledge. You may be on an intellectual adventure that leads you to incredible understanding.

Body (Two of Pentacles)

As evident in the card, the Two of Pentacles is a juggler. When it comes to your physical maintenance, you might not be too consistent. You may start an exercise or diet regime but drop it after a few weeks. The waves in the background of this card confirm an undulating motivation in your physical upkeep.

Spirit (Queen of Pentacles reversed)

This Queen reversed implies being overburdened. Is your spirit burdened? Do you feel overwhelmed with spiritual responsibility and conflict? This reversed card also suggests an element of guilt in your spiritual life. Notice the Queen's head is bowed as if she is shamed or perhaps in contemplation. As an earth-affiliated card, this Queen suggests an imbalance between needing proof and relying on faith. Perhaps you struggle with dogma because you cannot physically prove the existence of the spirit.

Corrective action for the mind (Two of Wands)

This card is a response to the "Mind" card position. As the Wheel of Fortune card indicated a whirlwind state of mind, the Two of Wands recommends you pick an object of focus. The figure holds a globe in his hand and this is his center of concentration. Perhaps your mind would be better served focusing on a worthy global cause or charity. Helping others in need or helping the environment is a brilliant way to gain mental clarity because you are focused on a goal. Wands are symbolic of creativity, passion, and social interaction. The Two of Wands recommends you pick a creative activity and run with it. This is also a card of travel. Take this into consideration. Perhaps travel will ease your wildly wheeling mind.

You're a smart cookie. You know that consulting your Tarot cards is a great way to get a good read on your health. But you also know consulting your health practitioner if you have real health concerns is the best course of action. The Tarot can be a vital part of a full, balanced life—but don't forget that proper self-care and health check-ups are also key for a harmonious life.

Corrective action for the body (Ten of Cups)

As seen in the "Body" position (Two of Pentacles), there is some juggling going on with your physical status. The Ten of Cups recommends stabilizing the ups and downs by appreciating the value of relationships. This card points to cherished moments with friends and family. It also suggests healing through your environment. Try to beautify your surroundings to enhance a sense of calm and tranquility. The rainbow in the card is symbolic of attuning your energies. Consider chakra balancing and holistic healing techniques.

Corrective action for the spirit (Queen of Swords)

This card answers the "Spirit" position (Queen of Pentacles, reversed). It recommends re-establishing spiritual balance. This card represents being in a position of power and influence. In essence, the message of this card is: "Let your spirit have the throne of your life." The Queen of Swords encourages you to give your spirit permission to be powerful. The single sword held by the Queen is symbolic of single-minded focus. This implies increasing spiritual focus. Consider starting (or redoubling) a meditation regimen. It's noteworthy that Queens were drawn for both the "Spirit" and its "Corrective Action" response. Queens are intuitive, nurturing, supportive energy. This implies relying on intuition more to achieve spiritual balance and renewal.

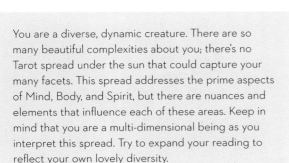

You are a diverse, dynamic creature. There are so many beautiful complexities about you; there's no Tarot spread under the sun that could capture your many facets. This spread addresses the prime aspects of Mind, Body, and Spirit, but there are nuances and elements that influence each of these areas. Keep in mind that you are a multi-dimensional being as you interpret this spread. Try to expand your reading to reflect your own lovely diversity.

APPENDIXES

FREQUENTLY ASKED QUESTIONS AND TAROT TROUBLESHOOTING

"Help! I'm stuck! What do I do?"

In an ideal world, you would never have to utter those words. Alas, the world and the Tarot are anything but ideal. This book addresses all the basics of the Tarot you need to know. Nevertheless, you're bound to get stumped at some point on your Tarot journey.

Anticipating that, here are some commonly asked questions about the Tarot with time-tested answers. You'll also find troubleshooting tips in the answers to help you in case you get stuck.

Q: *"I can't relax! I've tried to meditate. I've tried to get centered. I've been over and over these cards, but none of it makes any sense! What do I do?"*

A: Step away from the cards! From the sound of it, you've worked yourself up into a tizzy. This is only going to cause frustration and impede your ability to read the cards. Remember, the cards pick up your energy. If you're frazzled about not being able to relax, the cards will sense that and mimic your anxiety.

If you're having trouble relaxing, put the cards down and try again another day. Forcing it is never going to work. Eventually, you're going relax. Consider putting a deck in your purse or car so you'll always have it with you. Maybe you'll experience a calm interlude while walking your dog in the park. Capture that moment; take out your cards and do a simple reading.

Some people don't relax well, and not everybody is geared for meditation. If this is you, then ask yourself what you do to relax. Go for a run? Take a shower? Do those things first, and then approach the cards.

Q: *"I did an 11 card spread and got all green lights to 'go' in the cards. But when I got to the 'Outcome' card it clearly told me to not go forward with my venture. How do I interpret that?"*

A: There are several ways to approach conflicting messages in the cards. You can pull another card and place it on top of the card in conflict with the others. This additional card should give you insight as to the meaning of the odd card. If you're working with a big spread like this, you can do a follow-up reading to get more clarification. Do a simple three-card reading for summary and clear direction about your initial 11 card reading.

Q: *"I can't tell time! Tarot-time, that is. How do I clearly determine the timeframe in which my outcome will manifest?"*

A: You can establish time perimeters before a reading. For example, determine if you want to work with days, weeks, months, or years. Then use the number of the Tarot card as your answer. For example: You want to know when you'll get a promotion at work in terms of weeks ahead. You pulled the Seven of Cups, so start looking for a career boost within seven weeks. There are a few cards without numbers. Here are their values:

Ace = One
Page = Eleven
Knight = Twelve
Queen = Thirteen
King = Fourteen
Fool = Zero

Zero could be interpreted as either instant manifestation or that your desire might never manifest. It depends on what the surrounding cards in your spread indicate.

Another way to tell Tarot-time is by consulting the seasons associated with each suit. Here are the seasonal associations for each suit:

Wands = Spring
Pentacles = Autumn
Swords = Winter
Cups = Summer

Q: *"What do I do if I pull a card that seems to be completely unrelated to its position in a spread?"*

A: Many experienced readers will tell you there are no accidents in the Tarot. There is a deep, metaphysical reason that card landed in that position. Take a moment to question why you feel the card is unrelated to the position or your question. Nine times out of ten, the answer comes from having an expectation that the reading should go a certain way. It is imperative to remain objective when reading the cards. Keep an open mind and remain impartial. Don't become so attached to the outcome that you become blind to the answers.

Q: *"How long should I wait to do another reading about the same issue I've been having?"*

A: This is a personal preference. A week is a standard time to wait before returning to the cards if there has been no change in your circumstances. It's important to be aware of the dangers of "divination abuse." Divination abuse happens when a person becomes obsessed with getting answers from the cards. For example, you might become consumed with getting answers to a particular issue, consulting the cards every day, many times a day about the same issue. Doing excessive, consecutive readings like this tends to weaken the power of the Tarot. Eventually, the responses make very little sense. Also, obsessive readings imply a complete dependency upon the Tarot. Tarot can be an essential tool for clarifying life issues, but it's only a tool. Ultimately, you are the decision-maker in your life.

Q: *"I'm scared of the Devil and Death cards. There are other cards in the deck that are pretty creepy, too. Is there a happy interpretation for these cards?"*

A: Nobody likes bad news, but life is all about ups and downs. With every life there is a death. With every joy there is a sorrow. The Tarot wouldn't be very accurate in reflecting life's highs and lows if the deck only had happy cards in it. If you are uncomfortable with some of the cards, spend time with them. Meditate upon these cards with a goal to find inner peace about their message. For example, sitting with the Death card may ultimately reveal a message of transition. Perhaps you might come to understand that the Death card doesn't necessarily mean dead, done, game-over. It may reveal that death is simply a doorway into a new beginning. Here again, objectivity in reading the cards is key. Suspend your preconceived notions about what the Devil or other "creepy" cards mean. Doing so will enhance your maturity and broaden your potential for enriched readings.

Q: *"I'm not psychic. Don't I have to be psychic to read the Tarot?"*

A: It's true, some people are more naturally gifted with keen intuition than others. It's no different than some people having a knack for drawing or math. The truth of the matter is, all humans have some sort of psychic ability, even if it's just a smidgen. So the good news is you *are* psychic! You may find your intuition isn't as strong as you'd like. More good news—you can develop your psychic abilities. A daily meditation is a great way to enhance your intuitive perception.

If meditation isn't your thing, then engage in activities that boost your creativity. Creativity activates the imagination, and imagination activates intuition. Painting, writing poetry, listening to or playing music—these are all great for intuitive inspiration. Nature is another way to augment your intuitive abilities. Commune with Mother Nature every day with intent to connect your intuition with the beauty around you. Whether meditating, basket-weaving or taking a nature walk, be mindful about what you're doing. Attention to the energy around you and within you is key to developing intuition.

Q: *"Is what I read in the cards carved in stone? Can the outcome be changed?"*

A: No; and yes. Remember, the Tarot is an illustrated account of the human experience. There is precious little about life that's carved in stone, and it's the same with the Tarot. Life is replete with variables. Outcomes change and life is unpredictable. For example, let's say you take a different route to your favorite deli. This causes you to run into an old friend who introduces you to his best friend. As it turns out, you and your friend's best mate are a match made in heaven. You see how that one variable led to unpredictable changes? The Tarot can be remarkably accurate in predicting patterns, but outcomes (like life) can be flexible.

TAROT SYMBOLISM:
WHAT THE IMAGES ON THE CARDS MEAN

Almost every single object on a tarot card—from a person to a flower, tool, animal, and even color—has a meaning. Some, such as water, swords, and castles, appear on more than one card, and can have different meanings each time. Here is a list of objects you'll find on your tarot cards, and what they symbolize.

ACOLYTES (The Hierophant): The two kneeling figures are students of the church who assist in religious ceremony. They symbolize spiritual tradition, faithfulness, and obedience to god.

ALCHEMY (The Wheel of Fortune): The four alchemy symbols in the wheel are (from top moving counterclockwise): Mercury, Sulfur, Salt, and Ether. In alchemical wisdom these stand for Intellect, Emotion, Action, and Inaction, respectively.

ANGEL (The Lovers; Judgment): The angel is a messenger, a symbol of divine inspiration. Its presence implies our ability to answer a higher call. In the Lovers card, the archangel Raphael oversees creativity, health, and the healing arts. With hands extended, Raphael is expressing a blessing, as well as gifts of healing.

ARCHWAY (Three of Pentacles; Ten of Pentacles): Archways are symbols of structure, and imply an open door into new opportunity.

BANDAGE (Nine of Wands): Mending a wound—specifically, mental confusion or mending negative thinking.

BAPHOMET (The Devil): A mythological creature who is part man, part goat, and part male, part female. It symbolizes duality and the age-old battle between good and evil.

BATON (The World): Balance and harmony. They are divining rods; they conduct energy in beneficial ways.

BED (Nine of Swords): Unconsciousness and the dreaming mind. It may also represent sleeplessness or nightmares.

BEGGARS (Six of Pentacles): Beggars suggest giving to the poor and doing charity work.

BIRDS (The Star): Messengers that symbolize communication. (Page of Swords; King of Swords): Receiving news from distant places. (Queen of Swords): The bird brings a message that confirms what you have been thinking.

BISHOP (Death): An intermediary. He pleads for forgiveness on behalf of the people to insure entrance to heaven after death. He is also symbolic of the eternal nature of the soul—not even death can extinguish the spirit.

BLACK (Five of Cups): The figure in black with a down-turned head suggests a dark mood and loss.

BLINDFOLD (Two of Swords): An unwillingness to see the facts, or being blind to evidence; ignoring distractions. (Eight of Swords): Not seeing solutions or ignoring the facts. It may also imply introspection or going within for answers.

BLUE (Five of Wands): Communication, clarity and imagination.

BOAT (Six of Swords): Symbolizes an emotional journey; a crossing into new territory for a goal to purify the soul or cleanse your environment. The mother and child in the boat could be literal—you and your family are moving to a new location, or protecting something or someone upon which you place high value.

BOUND (Eight of Swords): Feeling powerless or having no control. Your hands are tied.

BRIDGE (Five of Cups): Crossing over an emotional gap in your life.

BULL (King of Pentacles): Fertility, dominance, provision, and sacrifice.

BUTTERFLIES (Queen of Swords; King of Swords): Transformation; time spent reflecting from within and bringing out revelations to the world.

CADUCEUS (Two of Cups): A symbol of medicine and healing.

CASTLE (Ace of Wands): The desire for stability. It is the symbol of your goals achieved. (Four of Wands; Seven of Cups): The home, security, and permanence. (Eight of Swords): The castle on a hill is symbolic of building high ideals or having high expectations; also home, structure, and foundations that seem out of reach. (Five of Cups): The castle in decline implies attention is required at home.

CAT (Queen of Wands): The black cat is a symbol of intuition. It represents curiosity and seeking out hidden solutions. The cat also encourages awareness and observation.

CHAINS (The Devil): The links on the chains represent each bad choice you make. Connected, they form your bondage into bad behavior, bad choices, and bad habits.

CHALICE (Queen of Cups): The chalice in the queen's lap is called a ciborium. It holds the essence of life. The queen is the protector of love, life, and all that is valuable.

CHILD (The Sun): The unclothed child is a symbol of innocence and simplicity; it reminds us to be more child-like and laugh more often. (Ten of Pentacles): Purity, innocence, and starting fresh.

CITY (Eight of Pentacles): The city in the background implies providing a service to your community or showing your creativity to a group.

CLIFF (Three of Wands): Standing on a precipice infers a higher view of a situation. The figure's stance also suggests inaction. (Seven of Wands): The figure's stance indicates defending your position. You might be on top, but you're fighting for status.

CLOTHING, FLAMBOYANT (Page of Wands): Extravagance and vanity. It may also hint to a talent for impressing or influencing others.

CLOUDS (Ace of Wands): Mystery, ambiguity and cloudy details. The hand thrusting out means taking action even if you don't have all the information. (Ace of Pentacles; Ace of Swords; Ace of Cups): The unknown. Use sharp intelligence to cut through the fog. (Three of Swords): Warning, hidden facts. (Five of Swords): The jagged clouds suggest erratic or tempestuous thoughts. Questionable motives are in the air. (Page of Swords): Pending events. (Knight of Swords): Jagged clouds suggest storms within the mind. It hints to erratic and chaotic thoughts brewing. (Queen of Swords; King of Swords): Thoughts brewing on the horizon.

COMPASS (The Star): The compass is an eight-pointed star, with each point representing directions. It is a symbol of direction and navigation.

COTTAGE (Eight of Wands): The small cottage in the background marks themes of home, security, and relocation.

CRACK (FAULT) (Seven of Wands): The schism underfoot implies divergence or contradiction—thinking one thing, but taking opposite action.

CROPS (Page of Pentacles): The crops in the field imply hard work to be done in order to receive material gain.

CROSS (The High Priestess): The equal-armed cross upon the Priestess's breast is symbolic of the importance of balance. Balance and harmony is at the heart of all understanding. (Judgment): The four directions, the four elements (fire, earth, air, water), and the four human touchstones (mind, body, spirit, emotion). (Ace of Cups): A symbol of direction (compass) and time. It suggests moderation and being in harmony.

CROSSED ARMS (Nine of Cups): Defensiveness, protection, or reluctance. It may also suggest satisfaction and contentment.

CROSSED LEGS (The Hanged Man): The legs in this position are symbolic of being at a crossroad and our mobility is impeded. Once the crux of the matter is determined, we become uncrossed and can move forward. (The World): A sign of completion; the ability to take action with confidence.

CROWD (Six of Wands): People in the background suggest a parade, procession, homecoming, celebration. There is fellowship and a following with you as the leader.

CROWN (The High Priestess): The Priestess's crown is a triple moon illustrating waxing, waning, and full phases. It reminds us to be aware of the importance of natural timing and patience. (Justice): Lady Justice wearing a crown implies truth is the "crowning glory" in the situation. (The Tower): Here the crown represents your mind, and thinking things through. (Ace of Swords): The crown implies mental sharpness. The mind is the crowning glory. Greenery in the crown is symbolic of planting mental seeds, observing what grows from mental investment.

CROWN OF FLOWERS AND LAUREL (Two of Cups): Victory and mental perfection.

CROWN OF STARS (The Chariot): The charioteer is goal-oriented, and the crown of stars symbolizes authority of the mind. It also suggests mental resources will illuminate the dark unknown's upon our path.

CRUTCHES (Five of Pentacles): The bandaged boy with crutches suggests setbacks, injury, and sustaining hardship.

CUPID (Queen of Swords): Love and compassion; someone looking after your best interest, especially in motherly concerns.

CUPS (Three of Cups): The raised cups suggest celebration, congratulations, and cheer. (Four of Cups): The cup forced from the cloud is symbolic of an opportunity, or a bright idea. (Five of Cups): Cups tipped over are symbolic of loss and negligent handling of resources. (Eight of Cups): The cups stacked at the forefront suggest love and emotional issues are at the forefront of life. (Ten of Cups): The placement of the cups suggest harmony in love and emotional stability.

DESERT (Page of Wands): Detachment. There is nothing of interest outside the self. (Knight of Wands): Vastness, open spaces, and room for expansion. (Knight of Swords): Isolation; a flat environment with no distractions.

DEVIL'S TAILS (The Devil): The two tails depicting flame and fruit hint to two of the seven sins: Gluttony and lust—a lack of moderation leading to personal bondage.

DOG (The Fool): Instinct, loyalty, companionship, and protection. In the Fool card, the dog represents a faithful presence guiding us and watching out for our best interests. (The Moon): Canines alert us to intrusions. They represent sensitivity to surroundings and outside influences. (Ten of Pentacles): Loyalty and faithfulness. Dogs represent being in a pack, like a family.

DOVE (Ace of Cups): Peace and news of hope. Birds are communicators.

DRAGON (Seven of Cups): Challenges and facing fears.

FALCON (Nine of Pentacles): Symbolizes having assistance in hunting for what you want in life.

FALLING (The Tower): The two falling figures are iconic of falling from grace. They represent loss of stability or status.

FARM (Ten of Wands): The figure moving toward the farm suggests taking resources and putting them to work for practical purposes.

FEATHER (Page of Wands): The red feather indicates a bright idea ready to take flight. A passionate objective is a motivating force.

FEET (Temperance): One foot in the water suggests clarity and connection with emotion. The other foot on the ground suggests being grounded and having solid footing.

FIRE (The Tower): The symbol of transformation, passion, anger, and energy.

FISH (Page of Cups; King of Cups): Expresses your emotion and intuition swimming under the surface. Fish may also point to unknown factors in life.

FIST (King of Wands): The king's clenched fist is symbolic of having control, authority, and being prepared to take action.

FLOOD (Judgment): Washing away of an old regime; a cleansing of what wasn't working in your life.

FLOWERS (The Magician): "Bloom where you are planted." Your life is a garden, tend to it so you can grow. (Two of Wands): The crossed flowers indicate purity (white) joined with passion (red). It hints to an even temper and good balance. (Four of Wands): The two women holding flowers are symbolic of spring, fertility, and savoring beauty. (Ace of Pentacles): The floral archway implies stepping into a direction of blossoming opportunity. Lilies are symbolic of promise, hope, and remembering the finer things in life. They also stand for fertility and purity. (Queen of Pentacles): The card is lush with foliage and flowers. This suggests abundance, growth, and flourishing prosperity. (Nine of Swords): The roses in the quilt are symbolic of balance of beauty vs. painful thorns. (Six of Cups): White flowers are symbolic of beauty in simple things and appreciating innocent times. The male figure relishing the scent symbolizes giving love, devotion, and appreciating beauty.

FRUIT (Three of Cups): Ripe fruit is symbolic of fertility in life. It suggests growth and bounty.

GLOBE (The Emperor): The world, and the Emperor's rule over it. In his hand, it implies concern and overseeing the welfare of the world though generosity. It is also a symbol of wholeness of community. (Two of Wands): Having the world in the palm of your hand. It alludes to a global, holistic view and to seeing the big picture.

GOAT (Queen of Pentacles): The goat on the throne is a symbol of fertility. It is also a symbol of sacrifice.

GOBLETS (Temperance): The goblets depict the flow of life. The action implies our getting just the right energetic mix for a complete life. (Seven of Cups): The head in the goblet is a sign of mental power, or that you are holding a memory of someone.

GRAPE LEAVES (King of Pentacles): Fertility, growth, and abundance.

GRAPES (Nine of Pentacles): The lush clusters of grapes in full ripeness suggests maturity and a time of enjoyment.

GRAPEVINES (Seven of Pentacles): Prosperity, celebration, and fertility. Pentacles positioned inside the grapevines implies a cash crop and harvesting value.

GREENERY (Four of Wands): The canopy of flowers and greenery resembles an archway. It is an invitation to step into celebration, growth and joy.

HALO (The Hanged Man): Enlightenment or epiphany has occurred. We suddenly realize what got us hung up in the first place.

HAMMER (Three of Pentacles): Force, action, industry, and creativity; chiseling out your way in life. (Eight of Pentacles): The act of hammering is a sign of getting your point across and/or getting the job done.

HAND (The Magician): The Magician's hand position symbolizes our connection between heaven and earth. In essence, they signal our ability to be "high minded" while staying grounded. (The Hierophant): The hand and fingers position are symbolic of benediction—a sign of blessing. The hand pointing to heaven signifies spiritual well-being and seeking spiritual guidance. (The Hanged Man): Hands behind the back suggests an inability to manipulate the situation. Manual force will not work to resolve problems. (Ace of Wands; Ace of Pentacles; Ace of Swords; Ace of Cups): Symbol of of action, initiation, and assertiveness. It also represents giving and/or receiving. (Ten of Swords): The hand is in a position of blessing. It suggests a final surrender of problems to a spiritual, higher force.

HAT (Two of Pentacles): The high hat is a symbol of high-mindedness, mental achievement, and high ideals.

HEART (Three of Swords): Your core issues, your passion, and what is "at the heart of the matter."

HERMANUBIS (The Wheel of Fortune): Hermanubis is a cross figure between Hermes and Anubis, both gods of the afterlife. It symbolizes the cycle of life and death or conscious and unconscious.

HILL (Four of Cups): The figure sitting on a hill represents you being aware of a challenge.

HOE (Seven of Pentacles): Hard work; rewards are equal to your efforts.

HORN (Judgment): An announcement being made. It is also a sign to "toot your own horn" and revel in your victories.

HORSE (Death; The Sun; Knight of Swords; Knight of Cups): The horse represents forward mobility. A white horse is an emblem of purity, power, and guidance, and moving toward emotional clarity. It is also a symbol of protection in the afterlife. In the Death card, a horse means moving from one dimension and forward into another. (Six of Wands): Freedom, momentum, and physical strength. Finely dressed, a horse implies championship and/or showmanship. (Knight of Wands): Taking charge, forward mobility. (Knight of Pentacles): A black horse indicates moving toward the unknown. Black is symbolic of mystery, secrets and shadows.

HUNCHED BACK (Ten of Wands): Back turned, shoulders hunched indicates laboring, and turning one's back on something.

INFINITY SYMBOL. See **LEMNISCATE**

IRIS (Temperance): Balance, hope, purity, and renewal. It is also a symbol of creativity.

JEWELS (Seven of Cups): A symbol of value and represent people or things that are precious to you.

JUGGLING (Two of Pentacles): Shuffling energy, balancing finances, or celebrating status.

KEYS (The Hierophant): Two keys crossed is a religious symbol of authority. They are the keys to the kingdom of heaven. In the Hierophant card, the crossed keys signify a spiritual mentor (priest, counselor) acting as an intermediary between god and man.

KING (Death): The downtrodden king illustrates Death's objectivity and inevitability. Neither status nor wealth can stave off Death.

KNAPSACK (The Fool): The basic needs in life, things we value and cannot live without. It also symbolizes emotional baggage and burdens we are not yet ready to release.

LANDSCAPE (Nine of Wands): The contrast in landscape from green mountains to gray slate represents contrasting origins, or shifting foundations. It may also imply moving to the city from rural farm life.

LANTERN (The Hermit): Represents spiritual or conscious insight lighting the way through darkness.

LAUREL WREATH (The World): Goodness, glory, and favor. (Six of Wands): The two wreaths signify a win for yourself, and another for someone you have represented or defended. (Seven of Cups): Winning a victory and perfection.

LEMNISCATE or **INFINITY SYMBOL** (The Magician): Indicates perpetual motion and an unfettered stream of consciousness. It reminds us the powerful, infinite influence of our mental focus. (Strength): Above-head represents continuity of thought. It also symbolizes balance, and flow of energy. It suggests constancy and stability in dealing with conflict. (The World): The red lemniscate represents knowledge and energy as indestructible, and a symbol of the continuation of human spirit. (Two of Pentacles): Balance, consequence, and a never-ending flow of energy.

LIGHTNING (The Tower): A symbol of a flash of insight, or a sudden jolt from out of nowhere.

LILY PADS (Ace of Cups): Resting places that encourage you to rise above emotional unrest and be secure in your intuition.

LION (Strength): Primal urges, physical needs, and cravings. It represents our animal nature—the side of us that is quick to attack without thought. (Queen of Wands; King of Wands): Passion, fighting for your dreams, and symbols of protection.

LOBSTER (The Moon): As a water-dweller the lobster is symbolic of emerging from emotional depths. As a bottom-feeder, it reminds us to visit deep-rooted feelings for self-realization.

MERMAIDS (Queen of Cups): Deep emotional insight and the importance of paying attention to dreams and intuition.

MONK (Three of Pentacles): Progress in spirituality, devotion, and/or religious growth.

MOON (The High Priestess): The crescent moon at the Priestess's feet indicates having control over our secret thoughts and emotions. As a luminary in the evening, the moon represents the light of awareness illuminating the darkest parts of our psyche. (The Chariot): Time, motion and unseen forces. They remind us that timing is essential in navigating smartly through life, and to consider hidden influences when making plans. (The Moon): A symbol of intuition and introspection, the moon represents illumination and clarification, and indicates timing. (Two of Swords): Intuition, phases in time, and emotional influences. It also represents being illuminated. (Eight of Cups): Emotion; intuition; and time, like the phases of the moon.

MOUNTAINS (The Fool): Challenges and higher opportunities. They encourage us to reach for higher goals, move out of small thinking, and climb up to a higher mental vantage point. (The Lovers): The mountain between the man and woman represents the divide between the sexes. Unifying with our partner (or our divine selves) means we must conquer the mountain of separateness. The mountain also represents our corrupt nature blocking our joy. (The Hermit): The Hermit standing on an icy mountain top is symbolic of dwelling in the highest reaches of thought. He has high ideals, which isolates him from the rest of the world. (Ace of Pentacles; Ace of Swords): The mountains in the distance imply hard work and challenges ahead. (Page of Pentacles): The mountain in the distance is a symbol of climbing higher in life, and accepting new challenges. (Queen of Pentacles): The mountains in the background suggest overcoming past challenges to get to a better place.

NO SYMBOLS (Eight of Wands): No symbols on a card suggests self-inspection, inward focus.

NUDITY (The Lovers): The ultimate form of expression, nudity represents comfort with ourselves and being completely natural, of letting go. It suggests power in vulnerability. (The Star): A sign of self-honesty and transparency, symbolic of self-security and feeling natural in any environment. (Judgment): A fresh start, being reborn and having nothing to hide. (The World): The partially nude figure signifies self-confidence and being at ease with all facets of yourself. Partially robed is an indication of modesty, and conscientiousness.

OLD MAN (Ten of Pentacles): Tradition, lineage, and wisdom.

PATH (Temperance): The path leading to the "crowning light" implies taking high moral ground. It illustrates walking a moral, upright path.

PENTACLES (Ace of Pentacles): Earthiness and being grounded; all elements combined and working together. (Four of Pentacles): The pentacles are crowded or clutched by the man, implying possession, greed, or control of monetary flow. (Five of Pentacles): The pentacles in stained glass imply finding value in art or spiritual ideas. (Six of Pentacles): Pentacles suspended in the air suggest there are resources to be found all around you—not just in the typical places. (Eight of Pentacles): Pentacles pinned on the wall implies showing off your craft, artistry, or awards. (Queen of Pentacles): The queen looking at the pentacle indicates being pensive and contemplative about home, value, and earthy matters.

PENTAGRAM (The Devil): The five-pointed star is a symbol of harmony amongst the elements (fire, earth, air, water, ether). Inverted, it is a symbol of disharmony.

PILLARS (The High Priestess): The pillars of Boaz and Jachin mean "strong" and "established," respectively. The Priestess in the center suggests wisdom, perception, and intuition are the "glue" for a strong emotional foundation. (The Hierophant): The two pillars framing the Hierophant is a symbol of balance. They imply harmony between spiritual and secular (worldly) thought. (Justice): They frame the card to represent the foundation of fairness, truth and equilibrium. (The Moon): The two pillars between the path suggest duality, and moving between contrasting opinions.

PITCHER (The Star): You as a vessel of energy and potential. The right hand pours out creativity and contains conscious thought. The left hand pours out order and structure and contains unconscious thought.

PLATFORM (Three of Pentacles): The figure standing on a platform is symbolic of getting a "step up" in profession or status.

POMEGRANATES (The High Priestess): The fruitfulness of our subconscious minds. Pomegranates are symbolic of fertility. This indicates planting seeds in our subconscious, with the fruit growing out into our conscious life.

PREGNANCY (The Empress): The Empress shows hints of physical fullness, which may imply pregnancy. This supports the card's theme of renewal, feminine power, nourishment, and growth.

PYRAMID (Page of Wands; Knight of Wands): The four-sided structure leading to one-pointed focus is symbolic of building on a solid foundation to reach a higher ideal.

RABBIT (Queen of Pentacles): Being grounded, sensitivity to environment, and fertility.

RAIN (Three of Swords): Unrest, disturbance, and storms in life.

RAINBOW (Ten of Cups): Promise, hope, purification, good health, and balanced energy.

RAM (The Emperor): Assertiveness, determination, and leadership. The ram is also a symbol of Aries, the first sign of the zodiac, further reinforcing attributes of leadership, authority, and other forefather-type characteristics.

RED FLAG (The Sun): Passion and claiming ownership for what we desire most in our lives.

RIVER (Ace of Wands): Motion, direction, and the flow of life. (Eight of Wands): A channel of emotion, a stream of thought.

ROCKS (Two of Swords): Rocks in the sea suggest blockages in your emotional waters. (Eight of Cups): Jagged rocks imply challenges, a rocky road to travel.

ROSE (The Fool): A sign of duality. Life can be sweet, but thorny too. Appreciate the simple beauty in life. A white rose is symbolic of innocence, purity and faith. (Death): Simplicity. The five petals symbolize the five senses, and the centerpiece represents inner knowing. The rose stands for balance between life/death, dark/light, etc. This is illustrated by delicate beauty contrasting with thorns.

SALAMANDER (Knight of Wands; King of Wands): The salamanders on the knight's tunic symbolize fire, passion, and acting exclusively on instinct—a reminder to observe your environment and how it influences you.

SCALES (Justice): A symbol of balance. The preponderance of evidence leans to one side or the other. The verdict of an outcome is contingent upon whichever side the scales tip. (Six of Pentacles): Balance between give and take.

SCROLL (The High Priestess): Information, education, and perfect knowledge. The Priestess is the guardian of this knowledge, meaning we must be vigilant in our search and preservation of sacred wisdom.

SEMICIRCLE (Nine of Cups): Symbolic of luck, as in a horseshoe. It may also represent half-completion, not yet coming full-circle.

SERPENT (The Magician): Transition, power, and temptation. The snake constricts the Magician's core (solar plexus), illustrating moderation and clear judgment is the centerpiece of power. (The Wheel of Fortune): Recycling (renewal in shedding its skin), secret wisdom, and temptation. It also implies being grounded in shifting situations. (Seven of Cups): The serpent is a symbol of temptation, but also renewal as the snake sheds its skin.

SHIELD (The Empress): The shield brandishes the symbol for Venus and female energy, suggesting divine feminine power as a protective force in your life. This is also a symbol of motherhood and protecting the defenseless.

SHIP (Three of Wands): The ships sailing out in the distance imply saying goodbye, or letting go. (Two of Pentacles): Travel, news from abroad, and/or adventure. (King of Cups): The ship in the background implies travel. It may also suggest exchanging resources and ideas.

SKY (Ten of Swords): The layers in the horizon suggest drastic changes in the future.

SNAIL (Nine of Pentacles): Being grounded and sensitive to your environment. It also carries a message that says: "Home is where the heart is."

SNOW (Five of Pentacles): The people walking in the winter snow is synonymous with isolation and feeling "out in the cold."

SPHINX (The Chariot): Power and protection. These two guard the chariot, depicting protection on the life path of your choosing. White and black represents perfect balance in your choices. (The Wheel of Fortune): Sitting atop the wheel (north) the sphinx protects higher wisdom. The blue coloring suggests intellect, memory and knowledge of human nature.

STAFF (The Empress): Authority and governance. In the Empress card, authority is expressed as a strong female, maternal influence in the community. It also suggests protection of life. (The Emperor): Kingship and authority. The circle atop the "T" is an ancient symbol of heaven (sun) and earth (the horizon line) united. It is a symbol of balance. (The Hierophant): This type of staff is commonly seen in the office of the Pope and is the symbol of religious power. It signifies the holder's responsibility to tend to spiritual well-being amongst his/her congregation or community. The three horizontal marks represent the triune of spiritual wholeness (i.e., father, son, holy ghost). (The Hermit): In the left hand it is a symbol of control over the subconscious mind. It also symbolizes having a tool (a crutch or aid) upon a difficult path. (King of Pentacles): The staff topped with a globe is a symbol of power and authority. It implies influence on a global scale.

STAINED GLASS (Four of Swords): Worship within a sanctuary, or letting the light in our lives to enhance our vibrancy.

STAR OF DAVID (The Hermit): The Star of David shining in the Hermit's lantern is symbolic of illumination by faith.

SUITS (CUP, SWORD, PENTACLE, WAND) (The Magician): The four suits suggests we have all the necessary resources in life to accomplish great things. It also suggests we need all the proper tools to get the job done right.

SUMMER (Three of Cups): Festivity, warmth, and growth.

SUN (The Fool): A universal symbol of growth, joy, and hope. It reminds us to take risks and step out into the light so we can flourish and grow. The sun also stands for spiritual support and illumination when we need it. (The Lovers): An analogy for the warmth of love radiating in our lives, and represents spiritual light shining through the dark night of the soul. (Death): The sun between towers represents the gates of heaven. It is a symbol of hope and promise, and a message of renewal after the end. (The Sun): Healing, growth, and spiritual maturity. It radiates light upon issues that need to be exposed.

SUNFLOWER (The Sun): Sunflowers always face the sun, an analogy for the soul seeking the light of god. (Queen of Wands): Spiritual navigation, and seeking the light of inspiration.

SWORD (Justice): Symbolic of cold, hard facts cutting through the veil of mistruth, of unbending and piercing outcomes. In the right hand, it is a symbol of what is known—the facts that are in front of us. (Ace of Swords): Taking action and cutting through obstacles. Keen intellect and communication. (Two of Swords): Crossed swords suggest being of two minds about an issue. Investigate the crux of the matter. (Four of Swords): The positions of the swords suggest one foundational issue we are pondering, yet other mental points are interfering with our focus. (Five of Swords): The fallen swords with the two figures in the background suggest surrender or giving up, or perhaps a disagreement that leads to a parting of ways. The figure holds three swords, which might imply selfishness, greed, and taking without respect for others. (Seven of Swords): The figure dancing away with the swords means you are holding all the resources. It also implies running away with the spoils of war. The two swords standing while the others are carried away suggests leaving behind something in your absence. It suggests staying connected to roots, or leaving behind a legacy. (Nine of Swords): The swords in perfect alignment indicates an overwhelming intensity and focus in one direction, an attention to detail and orderly thought. (Ten of Swords): The swords run down the spinal column, which houses the nervous system. This suggests nervousness, and interference of foundational support.

TENTS (Seven of Swords): The tents in the background resemble a circus, caravan, or gypsy setting, implying a temporary residence, moving on, or a nomadic, carefree lifestyle.

TOMBS (Judgment): The tombs indicate a period of being in the dark and closed off from the world. The figures emerging from the tombs symbolize a breakthrough, victory and/or enlightenment. (Four of Swords): Resting in peace, meditation, and deep inward contemplation.

TORCH (The Devil): The torch is inverted because negativity prohibits the light of love and hope to shine.

TOWER (The Tower): The tower represents something built—a structure that has taken a lot of work to establish over time.

TRAVELER (Two of Wands): The figure is dressed in traditional travel attire and looking off into the distance, symbolizing an upcoming launch into a new venture. (Eight of Cups): The traveler with a staff indicates having support while moving forward.

TREES (The Lovers): The trees of life and fire are symbolic of fertility, temptation, growth, and passion. They represent balance between love and lust. (Four of Cups): The oak tree is a symbol of strength and growth.

TRIANGLE (Temperance): The three-sided harmony between mind, body, and spirit. Its position suggests maintaining homeostasis is the heart of the issue.

TUNIC (Three of Wands): The attire of a leader. It suggests power and authority over a community.

VEIL (Justice): The veil between the pillars illustrates veiled truth. In all trials, some details are left out. This reminds us to take all the details into account and make our best judgment with the facts we have available.

VEILED FIGURE (Seven of Cups): Implies limitless potential—possibilities are all around, even if they are unseen. It also suggests mental focus.

VILLAGE (Six of Cups): The communal environment suggests involvement in your community.

WALL (The Sun): A barrier we must break through to obtain the freedom and joy we deserve. It also symbolizes blockages that are behind us.

WANDS (Five of Wands): Crossed wands imply making contact, connections, and reaching out. Wand positions may also indicate defense or attack. (Seven of Wands): Wand position is one of deflection. This suggests staving off unwanted influences. The other wands indicate conflicting opinions, influences stabbing at your ideas. (Eight of Wands): Wand position indicates straightforward speech and thought, and balance, direction. (Nine of Wands): Wand position suggests ideas supporting your own, or, conversely, opinions contrary to yours. (Ten of Wands): The wands represent tools. All of them gathered in the figure's arms implies taking all the resources.

WATER (The Empress): Cleansing, renewal, purity, and the thoughts stirring beneath our consciousness. (The Star): A symbol of purification, hope, resources, and the flow of life. (The Moon): Reflection, emotion, intuition.

It reminds us to purify ourselves to become clearer. (Two of Pentacles): Heaving high seas suggests ups and downs in finances. It hints to unpredictability and/or emotional upheavals. (Two of Swords): The sea in the background implies an ocean of the unknown. A calm sea implies emotional stillness. (Six of Swords): The rocky waters on one side, and still waters on the other, implies conflict or being of two minds about an issue from which you want to flee. (Ace of Cups): Symbolic of emotion, standing for purification and clearing energy. It washes confusion away and stands for reflection upon emotional issues. (Five of Cups): A river represents emotional fluidity and allowing feelings to flow naturally. (Eight of Cups): Clarifying intuition, and cleansing emotions. (Page of Cups): Purification of feelings. It also implies clear insight. (Knight of Cups): The stream amongst dry terrain suggests a refreshing, nourishing element flowing through your life. (King of Cups): Water flowing suggests emotional freedom and purified intuition. Water is the king's foundation, implying control over emotions and ruling by strong perception.

WAVES (Knight of Pentacles): The red waves in the background can be construed as fallow fields, or a river of blood. Both indicate a warning or an ending.

WHEAT (The Empress): The harvest, and a common symbol in mythology representing fertility and abundance. Bounty, provision, and nourishment are all themes related to wheat.

WHEEL (The Wheel of Fortune): The spokes in the wheel represent a compass (north, south, east, west) and suggest navigating through the directions of life.

WHITE DRESS (Strength): Purity. It reminds us to purify ourselves to counteract animal behavior.

WIND (Page of Swords): Circulation and movement; the "winds of change" are at hand.

WINGED LION (Two of Cups): Pride in family, strength, and courageously rising above challenges.

WINGS (Knight of Cups): A symbol of taking charge of thoughts and putting them to work.

WOMEN (Three of Cups): The three women are symbolic of the three graces in Greek mythology: Joy, Charm, and Beauty.

YOD (Ace of Swords): The Hebrew Yod represents spiritual point of focus. Six of them is symbolic of connection to god.

YONI AND LINGAM (The Chariot): A symbol of perfect balance between opposites. It represents unification and harmony between male/female, sun/moon, life/death, etc.

ZODIAC (The Wheel of Fortune): From the upper-left corner moving clockwise, the four symbols are: Man, Eagle, Lion, and Bull. These represent the four foundational elements and fixed zodiac signs: Aquarius/air, Scorpio/water, Leo/fire, Taurus/earth (from upper left, clockwise). They symbolize balance and structure.

INDEX

A–B

accessing your intuition, 7
Aces
    Ace of Cups, 156–157
    Ace of Pentacles, 96–97
    Ace of Swords, 126–127
    Ace of Wands, 66–67
affirmation, 10
air element. *See* Suit of Swords
allegory, 6, 10
answers to inquiries, 194–197
arcana, 10
archetypes, 5, 10
author of the Tarot, 4

basic spreads
    daily encounter, 208-211
    modified cross, 216-222
    past, present, future, 204-207
    taking action, 212-215

C

card positions, 190–191
Career, Quick-Read Meanings. *See* Core
    Meanings
The Chariot, 34–35
checklist, reading cards, 198–199
cleansing the cards, 188
Core Meanings
    definition, 8
    Major Arcana
        Chariot, 35
        Death, 47
        Devil, 51
        Emperor, 29
        Empress, 27
        Fool, 21
        Hanged Man, 45

Hermit, 37
Hierophant, 31
High Priestess, 25
Judgment, 61
Justice, 43
Lovers, 33
Magician, 23
Moon, 57
Star, 55
Strength, 37
Sun, 59
Temperance, 49
Tower, 53
Wheel of Fortune, 41
World, 63
Suit of Cups
    Ace, 157
    Eight, 171
    Five, 165
    Four, 163
    King, 183
    Knight, 179
    Nine, 173
    Page, 177
    Queen, 181
    Seven, 169
    Six, 167
    Ten, 175
    Three, 161
    Two, 159
Suit of Pentacles
    Ace, 97
    Eight, 111
    Five, 105
    Four, 103
    King, 123
    Knight, 119
    Nine, 113
    Page, 117
    Queen, 121
    Seven, 109

Six, 107
Ten, 115
Three, 101
Two, 99
Suit of Swords
    Ace, 127
    Eight, 141
    Five, 135
    Four, 133
    King, 153
    Knight, 149
    Nine, 143
    Page, 147
    Queen, 151
    Seven, 139
    Six, 137
    Ten, 145
    Three, 131
    Two, 129
Suit of Wands
    Ace, 67
    Eight, 81
    Five, 75
    Four, 73
    King, 93
    Knight, 89
    Nine, 83
    Page, 87
    Queen, 91
    Seven, 79
    Six, 77
    Ten, 85
    Three, 71
    Two, 69
court cards, 16–17
    Kings
        King of Cups, 182–183
        King of Pentacles, 122–123
        King of Swords, 152–153
        King of Wands, 92–93

Knights
    Knight of Cups, 178–179
    Knight of Pentacles, 118–119
    Knight of Swords, 148–149
    Knight of Wands, 88–89
Pages
    Page of Cups, 176–177
    Page of Pentacles, 116–117
    Page of Swords, 146–147
    Page of Wands, 86–87
Queens
    Queen of Cups, 180–181
    Queen of Pentacles, 120–121
    Queen of Swords, 150–151
    Queen of Wands, 90–91
Cups, Suit of. *See* Suit of Cups
cutting cards, 189

D

daily encounter spread, 208–211
Death, 46–47
decks
    Major Arcana, 14, 19–63
      Chariot, 34–35
      Death, 46–47
      Devil, 50–51
      Emperor, 28–29
      Empress, 26–27
      Fool, 20–21
      Hanged Man, 44–45
      Hierophant, 30–31
      High Priestess, 24–25
      Judgment, 60–61
      Justice, 42–43
      Lovers, 32–33
      Magician, 22–23
      Moon, 56–57
      Star, 54–55
      Strength, 36–37
      Sun, 58–59
      Temperance, 48–49
      Tower, 52–53
      Wheel of Fortune, 40–41
      World, 62–63

Minor Arcana, 14–15
    Suit of Cups, 155–183
    Suit of Pentacles, 95–123
    Suit of Swords, 125–153
    Suit of Wands, 65–93
Rider-Waite, 8
The Devil, 50–51
divination, 10
dropped cards, 191

E

earth element. *See* Suit of Pentacles
Eights
    Eight of Cups, 170–171
    Eight of Pentacles, 110–111
    Eight of Swords, 140–141
    Eight of Wands, 80–81
The Emperor, 28–29
The Empress, 26–27
esoteric, 10

F–G

Family, Quick-Read Meanings. *See* Core Meanings
financial forecast spread, 224–229
fire element. *See* Suit of Wands
first pass (Inner World), 196
Fives
    Five of Cups, 164–165
    Five of Pentacles, 104–105
    Five of Swords, 134–135
    Five of Wands, 74–75
The Fool, 20–21
Fours
    Four of Cups, 162–163
    Four of Pentacles, 102–103
    Four of Swords, 132–133
    Four of Wands, 72–73

H

The Hanged Man, 44–45
The Hierophant, 30–31
The High Priestess, 24–25
how to ask questions, 192–193

I–J

initiate, 10
Inner World (first pass), 196
interpretation of the cards, 8–9
    card positions, 190–191
    checklist, 198–199
    cleansing the cards, 188
    first pass (Inner World), 196
    getting answers, 194–197
    how to ask questions, 192–193
    preparation, 188
    responsible readings, 200
    second pass (Outer World), 197
    shuffling and cutting, 189
intuition, 6–7, 10

Judgment, 60–61
Justice, 42–43

K

key questions. *See* keywords
keywords
    definition, 8
    Major Arcana
      Chariot, 34
      Death, 46
      Devil, 50
      Emperor, 28
      Empress, 26
      Fool, 20
      Hanged Man, 44
      Hermit, 36
      Hierophant, 30
      High Priestess, 24
      Judgment, 60

Justice, 42
Lovers, 32
Magician, 22
Moon, 56
Star, 54
Strength, 36
Sun, 58
Temperance, 48
Tower, 52
Wheel of Fortune, 40
World, 62
Suit of Cups
Ace, 156
Eight, 170
Five, 164
Four, 162
King, 182
Knight, 178
Nine, 172
Page, 176
Queen, 180
Seven, 168
Six, 166
Ten, 174
Three, 160
Two, 158
Suit of Pentacles
Ace, 96
Eight, 110
Five, 104
Four, 102
King, 122
Knight, 118
Nine, 112
Page, 116
Queen, 120
Seven, 108
Six, 106
Ten, 114
Three, 100
Two, 98

Suit of Swords
Ace, 126
Eight, 140
Five, 134
Four, 132
King, 152
Knight, 148
Nine, 142
Page, 146
Queen, 150
Seven, 138
Six, 136
Ten, 144
Three, 130
Two, 128
Suit of Wands
Ace, 66
Eight, 80
Five, 74
Four, 72
King, 92
Knight, 88
Nine, 82
Page, 86
Queen, 90
Seven, 78
Six, 76
Ten, 84
Three, 70
Two, 68
Kings (royals), 17
King of Cups, 182–183
King of Pentacles, 122–123
King of Swords, 152–153
King of Wands, 92–93
Knights (royals), 16
Knight of Cups, 178–179
Knight of Pentacles, 118–119
Knight of Swords, 148–149
Knight of Wands, 88–89

L

LBB (Little Black Book), 10
Little Black Book (LBB), 10
Little White Book (LWB), 10
love and relationship spread, 230–237
Love, Quick-Read Meanings. *See* Core Meanings
The Lovers, 32–33
LWB (Little White Book), 10

M

The Magician, 22–23
Major Arcana, 14, 19–63
Chariot, 34–35
Death, 46–47
Devil, 50–51
Emperor, 28–29
Empress, 26–27
Fool, 20–21
Hanged Man, 44–45
Hierophant, 30–31
High Priestess, 24–25
Judgment, 60–61
Justice, 42–43
Lovers, 32–33
Magician, 22–23
Moon, 56–57
Star, 54–55
Strength, 36–37
Sun, 58–59
Temperance, 48–49
Tower, 52–53
Wheel of Fortune, 40–41
World, 62–63
meditation, 10
Minor Arcana, 14–15
Suit of Cups. *See* Suit of Cups
Suit of Pentacles. *See* Suit of Pentacles
Suit of Swords. *See* Suit of Swords
Suit of Wands. *See* Suit of Wands

modified cross spread, 216-222

Money, Quick-Read Meanings. *See* Core Meanings

The Moon, 56–57

N

Nines
Nine of Cups, 172–173
Nine of Pentacles, 112–113
Nine of Swords, 142–143
Nine of Wands, 82–83

O

occult, 11
oracle, 11
origin of the Tarot, 4
Outer World (second pass), 197

P

Pages (royals), 16
Page of Cups, 176–177
Page of Pentacles, 116–117
Page of Swords, 146–147
Page of Wands, 86–87
past, present, future spread, 204–207
Pentacles, Suit of. *See* Suit of Pentacles
pips, 11
positions of cards, 190–191
preparation, reading cards, 188
projective hand, 11

Q

Queens (royals), 17
Queen of Cups, 180–181
Queen of Pentacles, 120–121
Queen of Swords, 150–151
Queen of Wands, 90–91
querent, 11
questions, how to ask, 192–193
Quick-Read Meanings. *See* Core Meanings

R

reading cards, 187–200
card positions, 190–191
checklist, 198–199
cleansing the cards, 188
first pass (Inner World), 196
getting answers, 194–197
how to ask questions, 192–193
preparation, 188
responsible readings, 200
second pass (Outer World), 197
shuffling and cutting, 189
receptive hand, 11
responsible readings, 200
reverse position cards, interpretation, 8, 191
Major Arcana. *See* Major Arcana
Suit of Cups. *See* Suit of Cups
Suit of Pentacles. *See* Suit of Pentacles
Suit of Swords. *See* Suit of Swords
Suit of Wands. *See* Suit of Wands
Rider-Waite decks, 8
royals, 16–17
Kings
King of Cups, 182–183
King of Pentacles, 122–123
King of Swords, 152–153
King of Wands, 92–93
Knights
Knight of Cups, 178–179
Knight of Pentacles, 118–119
Knight of Swords, 148–149
Knight of Wands, 88–89
Pages
Page of Cups, 176–177
Page of Pentacles, 116–117
Page of Swords, 146–147
Page of Wands, 86–87
Queens
Queen of Cups, 180–181
Queen of Pentacles, 120–121
Queen of Swords, 150–151
Queen of Wands, 90–91

S

second pass (Outer World), 197
Sevens
Seven of Cups, 168–169
Seven of Pentacles, 108–109
Seven of Swords, 138–139
Seven of Wands, 78–79
shuffling cards, 189
significator, 11
Sixes
Six of Cups, 166–167
Six of Pentacles, 106–107
Six of Swords, 136–137
Six of Wands, 76–77
smudging, 11
specific question spreads
financial forecast spread, 224-229
love and relationship spread, 230-237
whole health report spread, 238-243
spread, 11
basic, 202-221
specific, 223-243
The Star, 54–55
Strength, 36–37
Suit of Cups (Minor Arcana), 15, 155–183
Ace, 156–157
Eight, 170–171
Five, 164–165
Four, 162–163
King, 182–183
Knight, 178–179
Nine, 172–173
Page, 176–177
Queen, 180–181
Seven, 168–169
Six, 166–167
Ten, 174–175
Three, 160–161
Two, 158–159

Suit of Pentacles (Minor Arcana), 15, 95–123
    Ace, 96–97
    Eight, 110–111
    Five, 104–105
    Four, 102–103
    King, 122–123
    Knight, 118–119
    Nine, 112–113
    Page, 116–117
    Queen, 120–121
    Seven, 108–109
    Six, 106–107
    Ten, 114–115
    Three, 100–101
    Two, 98–99
Suit of Swords (Minor Arcana), 15, 125–153
    Ace, 126–127
    Eight, 140–141
    Five, 134–135
    Four, 132–133
    King, 152–153
    Knight, 148–149
    Nine, 142–143
    Page, 146–147
    Queen, 150–151
    Seven, 138–139
    Six, 136–137
    Ten, 144–145
    Three, 130–131
    Two, 128–129
Suit of Wands (Minor Arcana), 15, 65–93
    Ace, 66–67
    Eight, 80–81
    Five, 74–75
    Four, 72–73
    King, 92–93
    Knight, 88–89
    Nine, 82–83
    Page, 86–87
    Queen, 90–91
    Seven, 78–79
    Six, 76–77

Ten, 84–85
Three, 70–71
Two, 68–69
The Sun, 58–59
Swords, Suit of. *See* Suit of Swords

T

taking action spread, 212-215
Tarot as an allegory, 6
Temperance, 48–49
Tens
    Ten of Cups, 174–175
    Ten of Pentacles, 114–115
    Ten of Swords, 144–145
    Ten of Wands, 84–85
Threes
    Three of Cups, 160–161
    Three of Pentacles, 100–101
    Three of Swords, 130–131
    Three of Wands, 70–71
The Tower, 52–53
trumps, 11
two-step approach, seeking answers, 194–195
Twos
    Two of Cups, 158–159
    Two of Pentacles, 98–99
    Two of Swords, 128–129
    Two of Wands, 68–69

U–V

upright cards, interpretation, 8
    Major Arcana. *See* Major Arcana
    Suit of Cups. *See* Suit of Cups
    Suit of Pentacles. *See* Suit of Pentacles
    Suit of Swords. *See* Suit of Swords
    Suit of Wands. *See* Suit of Wands

W–X–Y–Z

Waite, Arthur Edward, 8
Wands, Suit of. *See* Suit of Wands
water element. *See* Suit of Cups
Wheel of Fortune, 40–41
whole health report spread, 238-243
The World, 62–63